Beyond Da Vinci

Beyond Da Vinci

GREG JONES

SEABURY BOOKS • NEW YORK

ISBN: 1-59627-000-4

Seabury Books
Church Publishing Incorporated
445 Fifth Ave
New York, NY 10016

For Melanie and Coco

Acknowledgments

My wife, Melanie, provided invaluable understanding and encouraged me from the start. In many ways, she launched this project when she said to me last year, "My friend wants to talk to you about this new book called *The Da Vinci Code*. She's really interested in it but has some *serious* questions." She and a cadre of powerful, spiritual women are the reason I was emboldened and encouraged to write this book. This group includes my agent, Kathleen Davis Niendorff, who helped me take this book from proposal to manuscript, as well as the Rev. Cathie Caimano and the Rev. Dr. Susan Barnes who helped me to shape my thoughts in no small way.

Dean H. King and Jessica King have been extremely helpful to me by lending their writing and publishing expertise. Truly if it were not for them, again, I would not have written this book. Many thanks go as well to Professor Deirdre Good and others on the faculty at General Theological Seminary in New York City. I thank the staff and people of St. James's Episcopal Church in Richmond for helping me to get this project started through a retreat I led on the subject, and for supporting me as I worked on the research and manuscript.

Thanks to the Rev. Randy Hollerith and the Rev. Dana Corsello, as well as to Mr. Andrew Corsello — good friends whose refined theological judgment was incredibly helpful in putting this book together. Union Theological Seminary in Richmond was invaluable; the staff tolerated my lengthy stays in their excellent research library where most of this book was actually typed on my trusty old laptop.

My thanks to everyone at Church Publishing who made the writing of this book possible, especially to Cynthia Shattuck, my editor, who believed in this project.

I must thank Eric A. Von Salzen, my godfather, who spent incalculable hours on this project as my lead researcher, editorial consultant, and companion along the way. His training as a lawyer, writer, and Christian educator, combined with his gentle spirit, created a literary ally without whom I would never have completed this book.

Many thanks to my parents, Sam and Helen, who taught me to read and question everything — and who gave me twenty years' worth of expensive schooling! And special thanks to my late grandparents, whose talents formed the context of my early life: Kathleen and Joe, starving artists; Shep, university professor and Middle East expert; Nana — author, survivor, and spiritual seeker; and Grandy — psychiatrist, gardener, and wit.

Table of Contents

Foreword by Dean King

We live in an age fascinated with history. Our picture of the past is no longer solely entrusted to the hands of meticulous, too often exhaustive academics. This has its advantages and disadvantages.

Talented, serious writers, such as Caroline Alexander, Nathaniel Philbrick, Charles Slack, and Dava Sobel, are tackling everything from polar exploration to the vulcanization of rubber in engaging ways and finding devoted readerships. New readers mean more books shining light into the nooks and crannies of history, and so it goes.

Even historical fiction, the bastard son of the literary world, long notorious for its bodice rippers and swashbuckling malarkey, has come into its own. Combining careful scholarship with the methods of fiction to better reveal the past, writers such as Mary Renault, George Garrett, and Umberto Eco brought respectability to the genre and added greatly to our understanding of bygone eras.

Patrick O'Brian's Aubrey-Maturin series, called by the *New York Times* in 1991, "the best historical novels ever written," carried the genre to new heights. O'Brian's stories are so meticulously crafted that even Oxford dons stand in awe and cherish his re-creations of life in the early nineteenth century.

At its highest level, literature conveys profound, philosophical truth about morality, spiritual life, or the nature of love, friendship, or existence. Less ambitious works merely entertain or at least distract us from our daily worries, providing us with an escape into a more exciting world. Much latitude is allowed the fiction writer, whether of the higher or lower form, both in where he finds his sources and what he does with them.

William Faulkner once said, "The writer's only responsibility is to his art. He will be completely ruthless if he is a good one. . . . If a writer has to rob his mother, he will not hesitate." And plenty have robbed history to write great works of fiction. But when they do they must get the story straight. There can be no leeway in that regard, particularly if there is any claim to historical accuracy. When works purport to recount true facts from the past, they must do just that.

Writing standards in popular history and historical fiction have for the most part risen, and consequently more people are now learning more history outside the classroom. Identifying which works have historical merit and which simply use the veneer of history, the romance of ages past, to tell a good — if inaccurate — yarn has become all the more important.

Sparked by his reading of The Da Vinci Code, Greg Jones had grave misgivings about the scholarship that informed this immensely popular novel. He had grave misgivings about the vast number of people who might color their views of the very nature of Christianity from the "facts" as portrayed there. In Beyond Da Vinci, Jones does a convincing job of taking on those "facts" and does a noble job of extending the conversation. The result is a cogent description of the real facts about Christianity and Christian scholarship from an open-minded but rigorous priest and scholar.

In setting the historical record straight, *Beyond Da Vinci* restores the grace to the mother robbed.

—Dean King
author of *Patrick O'Brian: A Life* and
Skeletons on the Zahara

Introduction

*T*he *Da Vinci Code* is more than a novel — it is pop mythology. The author, Dan Brown, has concocted a thoroughly addictive mythological opiate for his readers, and they are hooked. People can't seem to get enough of the book's secret blend of esoteric ingredients like the Holy Grail, Leonardo da Vinci, Gnosticism, and Mary Magdalene. And by stirring the public's imagination, *The Da Vinci Code* has succeeded in opening their pocket-books. As such it may be the most influential work of pop mythology in recent history, as well as one of the most misleading.

Certainly the impact of the book is enormous. From an economic standpoint the book is a commercial phenomenon, with six million hardback copies in print less than a year after publication. That impact will only grow with its eventual release in paperback and Columbia Pictures' global release of Ron Howard's film version in 2005. National booksellers report that *The Da Vinci Code* has spawned an enormous increase in the sales of books with related themes.

My concern is the book's influence beyond the sales figures. I am troubled by its impact on the minds of its millions of readers and their religious, historical, and intellectual understanding. The vast commercialization of the book's intellectual property only underscores the point that the book's controversial claims of fact are deeply interesting to people. And because "everybody is reading it," everybody wants to know one thing: "Is it true?"

People want to know if the book is true because in no uncertain terms it claims to be based on facts and good scholarship. If it is true in its most basic assertions, then everything Christians believe is false. Many readers realize this, and they are unsettled by the possibility that everything they ever heard about Christianity was untrue. They are going around looking for some answers, and that is why this book was written.

My problem with *The Da Vinci Code* started the summer of 2003, shortly after the book came out. A highly educated and prominent national advertising executive who goes to my church had read the book a few weeks after its release, and it left her troubled. She asked me point blank, "Is it all true?" As we were sitting by the pool one day, she said, "I'm reading *The Da Vinci Code*, and I can't put it down." Then she said, quite naturally, "I didn't know that Constantine invented the divinity of Christ and created the Bible in the fourth century. Is that true?" As a vice-president for marketing and planning, she is paid a fortune to predict cultural trends, and she is normally months ahead of the cultural mainstream. Knowing this, I realized a problem was on the horizon.

And my foreboding came true. As the year rolled on, more and more people came up to me and asked me the same kinds of questions. It was no longer a person here or there, but whole groups of people who asked me to speak with them about their concerns. Therefore, I realized I needed to give these people well-researched answers, because the book is very convincing. Indeed, it is so convincing that Janet Maslin called the book "brainy," the *Atlanta Journal-Constitution* called it a "spellbinding re-examination of 2,000 years of religious history," and the *Chicago Tribune* said it contains several "doctorates' worth" of scholarship and ideas.

So I sat in my library and read. I ordered books from Amazon. I went to Barnes and Noble. I went to the research library at the local divinity school, where I reread dozens of books on ancient church history and theology as well as the Gnostic gospels and other "lost books of the Bible." I read books by the leading feminist scholars of our time. I even consulted Dan Brown's own sources. And what I found out made me mad.

It Misrepresents Christianity

Since I am an Episcopal priest, perhaps I'm too sensitive about Brown's critique of my religion. But you don't have to be a believer to get your facts straight. Take the great Italian writer Umberto Eco, for example. Eco is famously agnostic and critical of Christianity, and he loves to point out the church's all too historical pride and indulgence. Apropos of *The Da Vinci Code*, Eco is a real-life Robert Langdon, being a university professor of semiotics — not "symbology." An academic and author steeped in the study of language, symbol, and meaning, Eco's knowledge of the Christian religion and its history is also immense — even though he is not a believer. Like millions of his readers, I have learned a lot from Eco's best-selling novels, *The Name of the Rose*, *Foucault's Pendulum*, or *Baudolino*. His informed critique of Christianity and church history have challenged my faith in a healthy way, forcing me to think again about the less appealing truths of Christian history.

Perhaps *The Da Vinci Code* aspires to do the same. In the book, we are taught that the church is powerful, mysterious, and frightening — killing countless numbers of its spiritual enemies, including at least five million women falsely accused of witchcraft (*Da Vinci Code*, 125). But Brown's picture of the church is like a Gothic stained-glass window — drawn in thick leaden lines and large pixels of color. Except for one insulting aside about the Church of England (*my* church), the book makes no mention of any denominations within Christianity, as if the whole religion were unified under one spire. In the world-view of *The Da Vinci Code*, "the church" refers to all of Christianity, but it comes across looking like something out of medieval Latin Catholicism. For Dan Brown, the church and Christianity in general are uniformly clad in Roman dress and are peopled by a cast of characters straight out of Dante's *Inferno*. We encounter a religion run by albino monks, evil priests, and conniving Vatican prelates. While no denominations are mentioned, one small Roman Catholic traditionalist group, Opus Dei, is made to look like Al-Qaeda. In Brown's world, there are no Methodists, Greek Orthodox, or Quakers. There are no Pentecostals, Baptists, or Evangelicals. There are no Presbyterians, Lutherans, or Coptics. There are only Vatican henchman and Opus Dei assassins, all bent on solidifying patriarchal power for the church.

In the world view of *The Da Vinci Code*, moreover, Christians have been duped for centuries about the real truth of Jesus and Mary Magdalene. They have been forced by their priests to accept neo-pagan doctrines and scriptures allegedly invented by Constantine in the fourth century. And with no apparent exceptions, Christians appear to be all Catholic, violent, and sexist. This vision of the *"one, holy, catholic and apostolic church"* is kind of amusing, particularly if you hate Christianity, but it is a highly inaccurate portrait of a religion. Such glaring inaccuracy substantially weakens *The Da Vinci Code*'s claim that "nearly everything our fathers taught us about Christ is false" (*Da Vinci Code*, 235). In the pages that follow, I will look at Christianity in history, scripture, and practice, particularly with regard to the place of women and the sacred feminine.

The Da Vinci Code tells an exciting and violent story, but in my fact-checking I found that nearly all of its historical claims are highly dubious. With regard to its assertions about the history of the Bible, the definition of Hebrew words, and the sacred feminine in the Old and New Testaments, *The Da Vinci Code* is plainly mistaken and grossly misleading. As regards its supposedly historical ideas about Jesus, Mary Magdalene, The Gospel of Mary, and the role of women in pre-Constantinian Christianity, *The Da Vinci Code* offers nutty theories and fringe scholarly opinions as if they were well-established facts. In matters ranging from Constantine's influence on Christian thought to the alleged history of the Priory of Sion, *The Da Vinci Code* is largely built on recent works of pop mythology and pseudo-scholarship. Certainly, as prominent art historians attest, the majority of the book's key statements about Leonardo's lifestyle and career are overblown beyond recognition.

As Roman Catholic traditionalists and Evangelical conservatives have been quick to point out, Dan Brown's bestseller contains enough misleading statements to be viewed as a hostile attack on the faith of all Christians. But I do not intend to argue that *The Da Vinci Code* is "wrong" from the subjective perspective of faith or religious belief. I try not to get into the business of telling the world what is "right" or "wrong" in matters of faith — that kind of proselytizing is not my style. I merely intend to argue that the book is mistaken and misleading from the purely objective perspective of *facts*. In the following pages we will carefully examine *The Da Vinci Code*'s most important claims of fact, we will draw upon the insight of leading contemporary scholars, and we will separate truth from fiction as we go beyond *The Da Vinci Code*.

CHAPTER ONE

The Priory of Sion

FACT: The Priory of Sion — a European secret society founded in 1099 — is a real organization. In 1975 Paris's Bibliotheque Nationale discovered parchments known as *Les Dossier Secrets*, identifying numerous members of the Priory of Sion, including Sir Isaac Newton, Botticelli, Victor Hugo, and Leonardo da Vinci. (*Da Vinci Code*, 1)

The Da Vinci Code is part murder mystery and part quest for the Holy Grail. In order to solve the mystery of Jacques Saunière's murder, Robert Langdon and Sophie Neveu combine esoteric knowledge and cryptographic skills to decipher a set of clues left by the murder victim. In their adventure, the duo finds itself on the trail of "one of the oldest surviving secret societies on earth" — the Priory of Sion. They realize that Saunière was not only a member of the Priory, but was also its most recent Grand Master, an office purportedly held in the 1500s by Saunière's kindred spirit, Leonardo da Vinci. With the murder of Saunière and other key Priory personnel, including a nun at the Church of Saint-Sulpice in Paris, it appears that the Priory of Sion is under attack by its equally shadowy secret counterpart — the Pope's personal prelature, Opus Dei. On the very first page, *The Da Vinci Code* tells us that the Priory of Sion is a "real organization," and Leonardo da Vinci was one of its members. We also are told that Opus Dei "has been the topic of recent controversy due to reports of brainwashing, coercion, and a dangerous practice known as 'corporal mortification.'"

Langdon and Neveu discover that the Priory of Sion also possesses a shocking secret, powerful enough to overturn the teachings not only of the Roman Catholic Church, but all of Christianity. The secret is that Jesus of Nazareth was not the Son of God but merely a mortal prophet. He and Mary Magdalene produced descendants who perpetuated a sacred bloodline. Their descendants ended up in Roman Gaul and eventually intermarried with the Germanic conquerors of Gaul — the Merovingians – becoming the rightful heirs not only of the French throne, but of Jesus and Mary Magdalene. The book argues that this holy bloodline is itself "the Holy Grail," and it has been protected over the centuries by the knightly members of the Priory of Sion. For much of the book we are led to believe that the Roman Catholic Church has dispatched its Opus Dei hit men to eliminate the Priory once and for all.

According to Brown, the sect not only preserves secret knowledge about the "Holy Grail," but is also a goddess worship cult that secretly continues the matriarchal pagan worship that Christianity had suppressed. Indeed, Langdon, the Harvard professor of religious symbology, tells the reader that the Priory of Sion is "*the* pagan goddess worship cult." To give us a glimpse of the Priory's liturgy, Brown has Sophie Neveu remember that she once entered the secret basement of her grandfather's Normandy chateau and discovered her grandfather naked upon an altar having intercourse with a silverhaired woman, while a crowd of worshipers looked on (*Da Vinci Code*, 113).

Opus Dei is an actual organization, and Brown is correct in stating that it has been the topic of controversy for many years. While some of its members have gone to the pietistic extremes described in *The Da Vinci Code*, the group is primarily criticized for its historical affiliation with fascist regimes in Spain and Latin America, and its opposition to Roman Catholic reform movements. One prominent scholar of Latin American Studies calls the organization an extremely "retrogressive force in Latin American affairs." Larry Birns, Director of the Council on Hemispheric Affairs in Washington, D.C., told me in an interview that from its founding in Franco's Spain, Opus Dei has been intimately involved with some of the world's worst fascist regimes — in Spain, Chile, Argentina, and El Salvador. Interestingly, many of those regimes murdered their liberal Roman Catholic clergy. *Newsweek* religion writer Kenneth Woodward has called Opus Dei a "shadowy church within the church." [1]

Because I am no friend of Opus Dei's theology or politics, I am not particularly bothered by *The Da Vinci Code*'s treatment of Opus Dei. They are a real group, with a checkered history, and they can defend themselves against *The Da Vinci Code*'s claims. Where Dan Brown really errs, in my judgment, is in claiming that the Priory of Sion is a comparable organization, in terms of power and ideological seriousness, which purports to know the "real truth" about Jesus and Mary

Magdalene. *The Da Vinci Code* wants us to believe that not only is this group real in the way the book imagines it, but that its supposed teachings are essential for persons interested in recovering the "lost sacred feminine" in Christianity. It is for this reason that we must go beyond *The Da Vinci Code* and examine the real facts about the Priory.

In light of my research into the Priory and its alleged secret dossier of ancient parchments, which mention the group's illustrious membership, I think the first page of *The Da Vinci Code* should read:

"**FACT**: The Priory of Sion described in this book is not a real organization. The parchments discovered in the national library in Paris were planted there in the 1960s and are phony. The history of the contemporary Priory begins in twentieth-century France, not eleventh-century Palestine. The entire concept of the bloodline of the Holy Grail which derives from the Priory of Sion parchments is a fraud designed to enrich its authors and those who believe them. The long list of illustrious Priory members is completely fake."

The Priory of Sion Fantasy

The Priory of Sion, the secret dossier of parchments, the bloodline of Jesus and Magdalene, and the list of illustrious Priory members are all components of a grand hoax which has fooled people for nearly forty years.[2] The hoax is built upon a legend created out of whole cloth in the 1950s by French hotelier Noel Corbu. Corbu invented a fantastic modern legend involving lost treasure, ancient parchments, and Visigoths and

Merovingian kings. Corbu used the tale to stimulate interest in his pseudo-historical tourist attraction in the French town of Rennes-le-Château. In the 1960s, a French con-man named Pierre Plantard and his associates wrote a manuscript based on Corbu's idea. Plantard had founded a small club which he called the Priory of Sion, and which was little more than a support group for Plantard's strange claim to be the true heir to the French royal line. In the 1960s, Plantard's club fabricated parchments and documents and deposited them into a not-so-secret dossier in the National Library in Paris. In 1967, Plantard's book was rewritten and published by a professional writer named Gerard de Sede. That book would spawn increasing interest throughout France in the late 1960s.

In the early 1970s an English film-maker named Henry Lincoln stumbled across Plantard and his Priory of Sion associates. Thanks to his connections to the BBC, Lincoln brought wider attention to the legend, culminating in the 1982 book *Holy Blood, Holy Grail*. That book did so well world-wide that it was followed by a sequel named *Messianic Legacy*. A decade later, new authors would expand on the material, writing books like *The Templar Revelation* and *Bloodline of the Holy Grail*.

It is out of these sources that Dan Brown has fashioned *The Da Vinci Code*. Despite his claims to scholarship, Dan Brown has not only perpetuated a popular myth, but by putting the popular mythos of the Priory of Sion into a blockbuster bestseller, he has canonized a tale which forty years ago existed only in the imagination of a few French con-men.

What is the true story of the Priory of Sion? There are two ways to answer that question. First, there was indeed an ancient order called the Order of Our Lady of Sion. This group was founded after the First Crusade, and it existed for many years alongside a more powerful organization known as the Knights Templar. Second, while there was indeed a real organization founded in France in the 1950s called the Priory of Sion, that group had no real connection to the original Order of Our Lady of Sion, or the Knights Templar.

A Brief History of Mount Zion

The Old Testament tells us that King David captured a pagan stronghold called Zion, and it would become the basis for his royal city. The royal city of David, Jerusalem, has been sacred to Jews and Christians ever since. When the Romans destroyed Jerusalem in the first and second centuries, the Christians living there began to identify the remains of their ancient hillside neighborhood as Zion. They remembered the Old Testament prophecies that a portion of Zion would remain. There, they would preserve the faith and traditions of the apostles for three centuries.

With Constantine's conversion to Christianity in the 320s, the lives of these Christians changed drastically. On top of their sacred holy sites, vast church buildings appeared for the first time. Until that time, churches were little more than houses belonging to faithful men and women. Beginning in 325, enormous basilicas were built by emperors over the places associated with Christ's birth, crucifixion, resurrection, and ascension. On Mount Zion a church was built in approximately 348. According to the diaries of pilgrims to Jerusalem in late antiquity, the church on Mount Zion was built on top of a house church which originally belonged to the apostle referred to in the New Testament as "James the brother of the Lord."

The New Testament and early church histories explain that James was head of the church in Jerusalem after Jesus' ascension into heaven. A fifth-century pilgrim to Jerusalem named Hippolytus of Thebes writes in his travel diary that James was installed as the church's first "overseer" or "bishop" at the house church on Mount Zion. The Roman Christian pilgrim Egeria wrote in her famous travelogue that James' "throne" was on Mount Zion. And finally, a prayer book from the mid-400s, the Liturgy of St. James, calls the Church of Zion "the Mother of all the churches." It would be no surprise that the mother church of all the churches was dedicated to the mother of Jesus Christ, himself the founder and head of the church. The church which stands on that site today is called the Church of Saint Mary of Zion.

A few ancient texts do not agree that the original site belonged to James, the brother of Jesus. Some claim the house church on Zion was once owned by John, whom the Bible calls the Beloved Disciple, and who is traditionally depicted in Christian art as a beautiful young man. If it is true that this was once John's house, it fits neatly with other ancient traditions that Mary lived and died on Mount Zion, in the house of John the Beloved Disciple.

Interestingly, in the early 400s Christians in Jerusalem began to associate the Church of Zion with the Last Supper. As such, it would have been a highly valuable sacred site to the Christian community. It was a very popular site with pilgrims and a number of monasteries and convents were built near the church. The large Roman church on Mount Zion enjoyed three centuries of protection by the Byzantine emperors who ruled Jerusalem until the seventh century. The church on Mount Zion was damaged by Persians in 614, and again by Arabs in 965, but likely was still there when the Turks conquered Palestine in the late eleventh century and began to make life much harder on the local Christian community.

The First Crusade

In 1095, the Byzantine emperor sent an emissary to Rome begging for help in reclaiming the holy city from Muslim control. At the same time, a charismatic French monk named Peter the Hermit went around Europe stirring up concern for the Christians of the Holy Land. At the Council of Clermont, Pope Urban II called for a vast crusade to reclaim for Christendom the holy places of Jesus' life, death, and resurrection. While the pope certainly was worried about Muslim occupation of the holy sites, Urban II saw something more in the offing. He realized that in the liberation of Jerusalem he could finally control those sites most sacred to Christians. After centuries of rivalry between the many ancient apostolic churches in both the West and the East, the bishop of Rome saw a chance to claim primacy over all the churches of Christianity, not just the churches of western Europe.

Moreover, from the pope's perspective, the crusade offered a chance to end the constant warfare that characterized Latin Christendom. Since the fall of the Roman West in the fifth century, the petty lords of western Europe were constantly warring with one another. Despite periods of some unification —

notably under the Merovingian and then Carolingian rulers, who consolidated an enormous Frankish empire — Latin Christendom was a most brutal and fragmented constellation of feudal interests. Pope Urban II argued that the various nations of Christendom ought to be unified against the Turks. The call was heeded, and an enormous army headed East.

The First Crusade was led by several dukes and counts of western Europe, and no small number of monks, priests, and bishops, too. One of the crusaders who would be idealized by medieval writers was Godfrey of Bouillon. The duke of Lower Lorraine, Godfrey of Bouillon sold castles, towns, lands, and even titles to go on the First Crusade. Some were even sold to the church. In 1099 the largely French ensemble of crusaders conquered Jerusalem. As the many dukes and counts jockeyed for position, Godfrey of Bouillon, a distant descendant of the Merovingian kings, was finally selected as the titular leader of the new Kingdom of Jerusalem, and he was given the title "Defender of the Holy Sepulcher."

Before Godfrey died, he signed a charter for a religious group which sought to build a church and abbey on the large hill outside the city walls.[3] The group called itself the Order of Our Lady of Sion, and they wanted to build on the site of the old church dedicated to the Virgin Mary and located on Mount Zion. The small order appears to have been quite similar to the several other small Augustinian orders which were created right after the First Crusade. These orders were at least initially founded and dedicated for the purposes of building and preserving churches on Christianity's holiest sites. Some eighty years after its founding, it appeared in a papal bull from 1178 that the Order of Our Lady of Sion possessed property in

Palestine, Calabria, and France. Apart from that we know little else. The Order maintained its abbey on Mount Zion until 1291, when the Muslims reconquered the region. The group appears to have merged with the Society of Jesus around 1617.

The Knights Templar

Twenty years after Godfrey of Bouillon and his men sacked Jerusalem and liberated it from the Turks, European pilgrims began to flock to the Holy Land. Not surprisingly, many of the locals didn't appreciate a European and western presence, so acts of terror and banditry against them reached new heights. The Templars were founded to protect these pilgrims against the Turks in 1119.

Interestingly, before the Turks took control, the Arab rulers of Palestine were generally charitable to Christian pilgrims, with one or two notable exceptions.[4] Sadly for the local Christians of Jerusalem, the Turks were far less tolerant. As newly civilized nomadic barbarians, and as recent converts to Islam, the Turks often acted with far less restraint than the Arab successors of Mohammed. The Turks bore little kindness to Christian travelers in general, and even less after their defeat by the soldiers of western Europe.

It is important to note that in many ways the Turks and the Franks, though of different faiths, had a lot in common: both were a rough people of thin civilization and little religious sophistication. By contrast, the Arabs and Byzantines, also of different faiths, were highly civilized people of deep religious sophistication. It is not surprising that the Franks despised the

Byzantines almost as much as they did the Turks, and the Byzantines often preferred Arabs to Latins. At any rate, it is appropriate that the Franks and the Turks fought one another so viciously — for they were each a highly violent and warlike people. As an illustration of this animus, William of Tyre recounts how thousands of Turks were slaughtered by the Franks without mercy in the streets and precincts of Jerusalem. On another occasion, a raiding party of Turks attacked Christian pilgrims on Easter Day, 1119, and three hundred were killed or captured.

The Templars were intended to complement the existing orders — especially the Order of the Hospital of St. John of Jerusalem, which sustained a hospital for pilgrims in the Holy Land, and the Order of the Holy Sepulcher, founded by the First Earl of Warwick, to supervise and protect the building and maintenance of the Church of the Holy Sepulcher. The last will and testament of King Alfonso I of Aragon in Spain, dating from 1131, illustrates how the orders were seen at the time. Having no heirs, Alfonso I left one third of his lands to be divided between the knights who protected the Holy Sepulcher, the knights who cared for the poor and the sick, and the Templars who defended Christians in the Holy Land.

Baldwin I, brother of Godfrey and the first titular King of Jerusalem, gave the nascent Templar order a part of his royal palace situated next to the old al-Aksa mosque on the Temple Mount. At that time, all that remained of the Temple of Solomon was the ground upon which it once stood. The Temple of Solomon had been destroyed seventeen hundred years earlier by the Babylonians, who plundered and removed everything inside. That temple was rebuilt fifty years later under the reign of the Persian emperor, Cyrus the Great, but it was later destroyed again and rebuilt by King Herod in the first century BCE. (Herod was not actually a Jew, but an Edomite who was appointed King of Judea by the Romans.) The Second Temple, as it was called, was again destroyed, this time by the Romans in the year 70. It was never to be rebuilt. Some believe that its contents were taken to Rome and still exist there in the Vatican vaults — surprisingly, this is not mentioned in *The Da Vinci Code*.

At any rate, because Baldwin's royal palace was located near the Temple Mount, the warrior monks took their name from its ancient association with the Temple. It is said that they were formed with the express permission to seek out and commission excommunicated knights, to admit them to the order after the absolution of sin by their patron bishop, and thus to discipline and convert the unruly rabble of rogues and adventurers who streamed to the Holy Land in hope of plunder and salvation. The order quickly fell under suspicion with church leaders, requiring that they solicit the patronage and support of the church in Rome. The founder of the Templars, Hugh de Payns, returned home to receive the support and blessing of the powerful abbot Bernard of the Frankish monastery at Clairvaux. The Templar order quickly grew in power and influence, thanks to the appreciation of the many pilgrims it protected, and Bernard of Clairvaux won acceptance for it. A council gathered at Troyes in 1128 to sanction the rule of the order. Forty years later, by papal bull, the rule of the order was clarified and definitively centralized under the rule of the Grand Masters in Jerusalem, and under the patronage of the Patriarch of Jerusalem.

The Templars rose over the following century to a position of enormous influence and power in the Mediterranean and beyond. In the East they dominated the Holy Land and crusader world; in the West, their power was even greater. Soon becoming more than warrior monks, they gained huge naval, financial, and political power. In many ways the Templars were like a modern-day multinational corporation, with their own churches, castles, ships, banks, and armies. We know that they had massive influence and holdings throughout western Europe in every major state. The last Grand Master of the Templars was Jaques de Molay, who came to France in 1306 with 150,000 gold florins and ten horse-loads of silver.

It is no small wonder that, with the royal households of England, Spain, and much of France owing either allegiance or money to the order one way or another, the Templars would develop some powerful enemies. It is certainly no surprise that a year after Molay's arrival in France, King Philip IV accused him and his knights of monstrous offenses against God and humanity, and appropriated a great deal of the Templar wealth in Frankish domains. The Templars were tortured, tried, and ultimately executed over the course of nearly ten years. At first, the campaign against the wealthy warrior monks was led by kings and secular rulers, but before too long it would involve priests, prelates, and popes as well. Some of the Templars' vast holdings were transferred to the Order of the Hospital of St. John, but most of their treasure was divided among the various bishoprics, abbeys, and royal houses of Europe.

The wealth of the order would not only found many a small kingdom and enrich many a church official, The Templars' legacy would also beguile and fascinate historians, storytellers, and balladeers for seven centuries more. One strand of the legend is that some of the Templars fled persecution in France, Britain, Germany, and elsewhere, and ended up in remote Scotland. It has long been part of established Grail lore, repeated in the pages of *The Da Vinci Code*, that the Scottish Sinclair clan, who were known Templars, had endowed Rosslyn Chapel and used it as a repository of Templar wealth and secrets.

Modern Dreams of Knighthood

Eight hundred years later, upon the fertile soil of crusader lore and legend, the Romantic movement would grow and spread across nineteenth-century Europe. A century after the Enlightenment, which saw the destruction of ancient royal houses and the birth of industry with its characteristically urban din, there arose a deep-seated hunger and nostalgia for the "good old days" of chivalry and legend. Writers, artists, and thinkers across Europe began to dream again of knights and maidens, castles and dragons, secret orders and sacred relics. The public became fascinated with the Age of Chivalry, and in churches, universities, and studios there arose an outpouring of things medieval. Popular books like *Ivanhoe* appeared in bookshops and lending libraries; Richard Wagner composed operas about knights and the Holy Grail. Even the Protestant churches of the West rediscovered medieval architecture and art.

The public also grew fascinated with the occult rites and rituals of Freemasonry, which was sympathetic to the ideals of the Enlightenment. The period witnessed a rise in the number of duly constituted and regally founded orders of chivalry as well. In England, for example, alongside the growth of its empire, new orders of chivalry were established to honor members of the new gentry and aristocracy. One ancient order, of which I am a member, the Order of the Hospital of St. John of Jerusalem, banished since the reign of Henry VIII, was reestablished in England during the reign of Queen Victoria. Elsewhere people sought to reconnect with a lost but glorious past. Even in America, college fraternities sprang up all over the landscape, each claiming some sort of secret origins, typically with a mixture of Masonic, Christian, and chivalric ideas and symbols. In the nineteenth century, pseudo-mystical groups arose like the Rosicrucians, the Order of the Golden Dawn, which numbered poet W. B. Yeats and his circle among its members.

An interesting example of this romantic nostalgia in early twentieth-century America is the importation and reconstruction of an English manor house in Richmond, Virginia. "Virginia House" was brought to the capital of the old Confederacy brick by brick in the 1920s by a rich Virginian who must have seen himself as a true "Cavalier." The building is many centuries old and was originally the Warwick, England priory of the Order of the Holy Sepulcher of Jerusalem. Virginia House is now a popular tourist attraction in Richmond.

The Treasure of Rennes-le-Château

Set against this Romantic backdrop is the strange case of a nineteenth-century French priest named Bérenger Saunière, who is central to the modern-day legend upon which *The Da Vinci Code* is built. Indeed, Dan Brown claims that everything he wrote about Jesus, the Magdalene, and the Priory of Sion is based on a set of ancient parchments supposedly discovered by this country vicar. The fact that the murdered curator in *The Da Vinci Code* is named Jacques Saunière indicates the degree to which Brown has assimilated the Saunière myth.

Bérenger Saunière was a Roman Catholic priest posted to a small country cure. During the political conflict which gripped France in the late nineteenth century — between Roman Catholic rightists and secular republicans on the left — Saunière profited greatly by taking advantage of the piety of pro-church rightists who sought to restore the French monarchy and keep the Roman Catholic Church established in France. Saunière made a fortune over a twenty-year period by selling masses to Catholics who believed a private celebration of the Holy Eucharist could buy them a special personal blessing. Most priests consider the peddling of the sacraments to be a disgrace to the church — but undeterred by shame, Saunière advertised the sale of masses in religious papers, magazines, and journals around the world.

Primary materials indicate that Saunière lived in poverty for most of his life except in that twenty-year period, when he made numerous improvements to his church, adding statuary, gardens, and art. Like the rich Virginian of the 1920s, with his dreams of knighthood, Saunière even built a medieval miniature castle he would call the Tower of Magdalene. In 1911, Saunière was inhibited from exercising his priesthood by the bishop of Carcassone for selling masses. While he was never reinstated as a valid priest, he did receive

Final Unction or Last Rites at his death.[5] According to financial documents, we learn that Saunière's estate was valued at
eighteen thousand francs by the Crédit Foncier de France in
1913 when he asked it for a loan in order to clear his debts;
he was offered six thousand. In 1917, according to ecclesias-
tical and government records, Saunière died as an impoverished debtor, transferring much of his property away from the
church to his maid.

Nearly forty years after the disgraced priest's death, his
faithful servant, Marie Dénarnaud, made the acquaintance of
Noel Corbu. Corbu was an intelligent if unsuccessful businessman, who looked after her, and in exchange received all of her
estate. He and his wife took ownership of the Tower of
Magdalene, and there they opened an inn. Corbu needed a
publicity gimmick to attract customers to his establishment,
and so he composed a story, which would be related to visitors
of the inn. He wrote out his short tale, and then recorded it
onto a tape which would be played for visitors. The story went
something like this:

In the fifth century, Rennes-le-Château was the Visigothic
capital of Razes — a city of perhaps thirty thousand inhabi-
tants. Until the Frankish conquest of previously Gallo-Roman
and Visigoth territories, the predominant type of Christianity
in Rennes-le-Château was Arianism, a sect that denied the full
divinity of Jesus Christ. The city began its decline in the thirteenth century with the Vatican's hideous crusade against the
heretical Albigensian sect located in the area. In the centuries
following the town's decline, Rennes-le-Château would have
been completely forgotten if Bérenger Saunière had not been
appointed to the village in 1885.

Bérenger Saunière was no more than a poor country priest for seven years, until February 1892. In that month, he asked for money from the town council to restore the church's high altar. When they dismantled it, the workers found wooden rolls containing scrolls in one of the pillars. The priest took them and stopped the work immediately, for something had caught his attention. The next day he set off for Paris. When he returned, he had the work started again to restore not only the high altar, but the whole church.

Saunière built walls around the gardens outside the church. He used a splendid Visigoth pillar as a stool for a stat-ue of the Virgin Mary. He had the rectory restored. Then, in 1897, he ordered the building of the mansion, the Magdalene tower, the gardens, the covered way, and the glasshouse. Saunière's life became luxurious, with guests and large dinner parties every day. He ordered seventy liters of rum a month directly from Jamaica, and his ducks were fed purely on biscuits to give them a finer taste.

When the bishop asked Saunière to explain his luxurious lifestyle, Saunière instead went abroad. The bishop grew angry, and in 1911, he accused Father Saunière of selling masses ille-gally, and forbade him to say mass anymore. Saunière went on saying mass in his private chapel and most of the villagers came to hear him. On January 22, 1917, he caught a cold, and died.

His maid took ownership of everything, but in 1947, she agreed to sell the buildings to the Corbus, who turned the priest's house into a hotel. A great part of the treasure was said to remain. Files in Carcassonne explain its legendary origins, which dated from the time of Blanche de Castille, mother of King Louis IX, who ruled France in the 1250s while her son was leading a crusade. Since Paris was not a safe location for the royal treasure, Blanche sent the treasure to Rennes for safe-keeping, and died shortly afterwards. All knowledge of the treasure was lost — until Father Saunière found the scrolls.

This is a good story — but remember, it is pure fiction. In 1967 the Vicar General of Carcassone issued a public warning that the whole legend was bogus, and a number of archaeological digs have been carried out at Rennes-le-Château to determine if there is any evidence of buried treasure. A good account of these activities can be found in *Mythologie du trésor de Rennes* by René Descadeillas. The first excavation of the church at Rennes-le-Château in the late 1950s found nothing. Another investigation was completed in 2003, and despite the popularity of *Holy Blood, Holy Grail*, which repackaged this story for millions of fascinated readers, nothing at all was found.

The Hoax

Despite the interference of the facts, Noel Corbu's fantasy about Saunière's treasure did not die out. It got picked up by another French con-man with grander hopes than simply creating a tourist attraction. The story of treasures and ancient parchments hidden in pillars became intertwined with a group calling itself the Priory of Sion, formed in 1956 by Pierre Plantard and André Bonhomme. Photocopies of the original documents show that the two young men registered in the French town of St. Julien-en-Genevois. According to statements made by André Bonhomme years later, in an effort to disassociate himself from the absurd claims of his former friend, the original Priory of Sion had nothing to do with Bérenger Saunière, Rennes-le-Château, politics, or secret societes.

Despite Bonhomme's claim of political innocence, his colleague Plantard had a long history of right-wing politics, anti-Semitic leanings, and a love of the esoteric stretching back at least to the 1930s. Notably, in 1936, the French right wing decried the election of Leon Blum as France's first Jewish prime minister, and the rightist Frenchman coined the slogan in those days, "Better Hitler than Blum." In 1937, Pierre Plantard actively recruited members for an anti-Jewish and anti-Masonic movement whose ultimate aim was to purify and renew France. A stated goal of this early group — which called itself "Alpha Galates" or "the First Gauls" — was also, strangely enough, the restoration of the Merovingian dynasty.

During Germany's occupation of France, Pierre Plantard wrote letters to the Vichy government aligning himself with their interests, and warning them to be wary of Jewish Masonic plots. In 1941 Plantard tried to form a group to be called French National Renewal. The German authorities — who shared the anti-Semitism but not the Monarchist Roman Catholicism of the Gallic right — refused permission for the group to be formed. A year later Plantard appears under the pseudonym, "Pierre de France," in an Alpha Galates journal. In that journal he writes: "I want Hitler's Germany to know that every obstacle to our own plans does harm him also, for it is the resistance put up by freemasonry that is undermining German might." The following year, in 1942, Plantard sought to found an order of knighthood called, again, Alpha Galates. But the Order of Alpha Galates was not properly registered with the authorities and Plantard was sentenced to four months in Fresnes prison. Plantard would return to prison in 1953 for six months for fraud.

The original Priory of Sion broke up in 1957, but two years later, in 1959, Plantard revived it with a small publication called *Circuit*. This little journal focused on esoteric material and right-wing monarchist fantasies, and in 1960 it ran a small piece on Pierre Plantard's psychic abilities. Concurrent to this, in the early 1960s, the Priory of Sion began to fabricate and deposit documents in the National Library in Paris. Included were false genealogies, papers written under pseudonyms but in Plantard's hand-writing, symbol-laden charts, and two enigmatic parchments which would become *Les Dossiers Secret* of the Priory of Sion.

These materials were completed before 1967, when Pierre Plantard finished a novel-length manuscript in which he outlined the whole legendary synthesis. Plantard was unable to find a reputable publisher for his manuscript, so he contracted with a writer named Gerard de Sede to rework and rewrite the material. Plantard brought in a third associate named Phillipe de Cherissey, who assisted with the project by creating a pair of mysterious-looking parchments — one large and one small. The Priory of Sion parchments were written in something like Latin and in an obscure character set, and they were decorated with curious arcane symbols. The book was published under the title "The Gold of Rennes," or *L'Or de Rennes*.

L'Or de Rennes became a primary source for all subsequent work involving the core Priory of Sion mythology. The book also became the sore point over which the scheme began to unravel — in France anyway. Shortly after its publication, a dispute arose between the three contributors over royalties. After the three quarreled over money, Pierre Plantard chose to make it known that the parchments published in the book were fakes. In 1971, Phillipe de Cherissey began to tell the world that he was the artist who created the parchments. In his book entitled *Circuit*, he brags about creating the parchments from his research into old manuscripts, themes, codes, and the like.

Amazingly, despite the unraveling of this hoax in the French-speaking world, British film-maker Henry Lincoln began to cover the story for the BBC. Lincoln's interest alone breathed new life into this increasingly stale material, and he found a new and highly credulous audience for it. His work perpetuated the hoax in small articles and films in the 1970s that formed the basis for *Holy Blood, Holy Grail*. Lincoln confesses that he received most of his key Priory of Sion information directly from Gerard de Sede and Pierre Plantard themselves.

Despite the popularity of *Holy Blood, Holy Grail*, which included photos and flattering text about Pierre Plantard, things would get worse for the man who wanted to be king of France. While Henry Lincoln was telling fascinated English readers about this "dignified, courteous man of discreetly aristocratic bearing," the French public was reading something else entirely. Writer Jean-Luc Chaumeil began publishing incriminating evidence of Plantard's fascist origins and his history of fraud and embezzlement. Because of Chaumeil's work and the resulting public humiliation, Plantard resigned from the Priory of Sion.

Plantard was extremely persistent, however. Although it seems hard to believe, in 1989 he came back one more time with still another version of the Priory legend and a revised version of the Priory's list of Grand Masters. It would be his final undoing. The new and improved list of Grand Masters included the name of one Roger-Patrice Pelat, a wealthy financier and prominent advisor to the French President Francois Mitterand, who was under investigation by the authorities for financial shenanigans. In 1993 Judge Thierry Jean-Pierre investigated the financial scandal involving Roger-Patrice Pelat. In light of the supposed connection to the Priory of Sion, the judge ordered the search of Plantard's house. This produced a hoard of Priory documents, some of which claimed that Plantard was the "true King of France." Plantard had to admit that he had made the whole thing up. The judge rebuked Plantard and ordered him never to involve himself with Priory activities again. Plantard himself died in 2000.

Interestingly enough, in the mid-1970s Plantard also adopted a surname for himself, styling himself "de Sinclair." Despite his pretense to be an heir to Godfrey de Bouillon, the Merovingian dynasty, and the Sinclairs of Scotland, Plantard's ashes are not preserved at Rosslyn Chapel. It would seem that his only lasting memorial will be in the pages of *The Da Vinci Code*, where we learn that character Sophie Neveu's true name is "Plantard de Saint-Clair."

It is unclear what the creators of the Priory of Sion were trying to accomplish with their mysterious hoax. It would appear that Plantard and his associates were simply trying to make a living, publish books, and establish some prominence for themselves in the esoteric circles in which they ran. It would appear as well, from his lifetime of work, that Plantard actually wanted to become the king of France!

At any rate, we have shown that what Dan Brown plainly labels "fact" simply isn't anything of the sort. The Priory of Sion is not a secret society founded in Jerusalem in 1099, but a con game started in France in the mid-1950s. The original Order of Our Lady of Sion was indeed founded in eleventh-century Jerusalem, but not as a secret society. It appears to have had almost nothing to do with the Knights Templar. Moreover, *Les Dossiers Secrets*, found in the Bibliotheque Nationale in Paris, was nothing more than a collection of forgeries planted by Pierre Plantard and his associates. It goes without saying, therefore, that Leonardo da Vinci was not a member of this organization — nor were Sir Isaac Newton, Botticelli, or Victor Hugo. The names of these illustrious persons were simply included in an ingenious membership list of the fraudulent Priory of Sion organization.

In the next chapter, we will explore the equally false claims made in *The Da Vinci Code* about Leonardo da Vinci, with a brief discussion of his lifestyle, beliefs, and work.

CHAPTER TWO

Leonardo and the Woman
at the Last Supper

Da Vinci had always been an awkward subject for historians, especially in the Christian tradition. Despite
the visionary's genius, he was a flamboyant homosexual and worshiper of Nature's divine order, both of
which placed him in a perpetual state of sin against
God....Even Da Vinci's enormous output of breathtaking Christian art only furthered the artist's reputation
for spiritual hypocrisy. Accepting hundreds of lucrative Vatican commissions, Da Vinci painted Christian
themes not as an expression of his own beliefs but
rather as a commercial venture - u means of funding
a lavish lifestyle. (*Da Vinci Code*, 45)

The artist Leonardo da Vinci is an important figure in *The
Da Vinci Code*. The book identifies Leonardo as "a well
documented devotee of the ancient ways of the goddess" and
as having been Grand Master of the Priory of Sion from 1510
until 1519 (*Da Vinci Code*, 97). Leonardo's supposed involve-

ment with the Priory of Sion is meant to lend an air of prominence and credibility to its ideas and practices. Moreover, Leonardo and his work provide one of the key points of the book's plot. One of Leonardo's paintings, *The Last Supper*, supposedly provides a clue to the identity of the "Holy Grail"; two other paintings, the *Mona Lisa* and the *Madonna of the Rocks*, also furnish clues in the scavenger hunt. In fact, Jacques Sauniere, the art curator whose murder sets the plot of *The Da Vinci Code* in motion, leaves a clue about his death by arranging his dying body in the position of *The Vitruvian Man*, a figure from Leonardo's sketchbooks. As the quotation above shows, *The Da Vinci Code* co-opts Leonardo as a standard bearer for the book's New Age ideas and anti-church invective.

Because the historical Leonardo is so important in the novel, I assumed that *The Da Vinci Code* would at least get right its most basic assertions about him. After all, Leonardo is one of history's most studied men. Dan Brown asserts in his acknowledgements that he did extensive research at the Louvre and elsewhere, and also had the help of his wife, an art historian. It is therefore unsettling that *The Da Vinci Code*'s historical treatment of Leonardo da Vinci is so full of errors. Much in the same way that its claims about the Priory of Sion are almost entirely based on questionable and even fraudulent sources, *The Da Vinci Code* makes highly dubious statements about Leonardo's lifestyle, religious beliefs, and artwork. For example, nearly everything in the quotation above — from his flamboyant behavior to his spiritual hypocrisy — is false or misleading. Similarly, the book's interpretation of *The Last Supper*, which is lifted entirely from Picknett and Prince's work, *The Templar Revelation*, is absurd. But what are the basic facts behind the myth about Leonardo da Vinci and *The Last Supper?* Let's go beyond *The Da Vinci Code* and find out.

A Sketch of Leonardo

Leonardo was born in 1452 in a tiny place called Anchiano, near the Italian village of Vinci. He was the illegitimate son of a minor local official named Ser Piero da Vinci and a young farmer's daughter named Catarina. Today, the artist is *popularly* known as Leonardo da Vinci, but this is somewhat misleading. Professional scholars refrain from calling him this because "da Vinci" simply means "from" or "of" Vinci, which refers to the artist's hometown, not his family name. Appropriately, art historians refer to him simply as Leonardo. I would not have known this myself, not being an art historian. But after having done some checking with actual scholars of Leonardo, it becomes particularly galling that the supposedly brilliant Robert Langdon character — a professor of religious art at Harvard — refers to the artist as "Da Vinci" throughout the entire book.

Even though Leonardo was illegitimate, he was nonetheless baptized into the church and appears to have grown up in his father's family. His father and his father's first wife never had other children, and it appears they raised the young Leonardo with them in their home in Vinci. As a teen, he moved to Florence with the family, and it was there that he became an apprentice in the studio of Andrea del Verrocchio, one of the great painters and sculptors of the Italian

Renaissance. An angel in Verrocchio's famous painting *The Baptism of Christ* has long been recognized to be Leonardo's contribution, and it was painted when he was no more than twenty years old. He continued in Verrocchio's studio for several years, and then became established as a master in his own right by 1478, at the age of twenty-six.

At the age of thirty, the artist from the town of Vinci did something remarkable. In 1482, he offered his services to the court of the Duke of Milan, Ludovico Sforza, where he would serve primarily as the Duke's military engineer. Leonardo designed and built cannons, siege engines, ships, armored vehicles, and portable bridges for the warlike duke. For the next seventeen years he was the Duke's principal military engineer, commissioned by him to design buildings and sculptures as well. Most notably Leonardo created theater designs, a model dome for the cathedral in Milan, and a huge bronze monument to the Duke's father, Francesco Sforza. He also completed a handful of paintings over the nearly two decades he served as chief weapons designer in Milan, among them *The Virgin of the Rocks*, several portraits, and *The Last Supper*. (We will turn to that great work shortly.)

While in the service of the Duke of Milan, Leonardo became acquainted with the great mathematician Lucas Pacioli. The Tuscan mathematical genius had been invited to teach math at Ludovico Sforza's court. The appointment may well have been made on the suggestion of the court military engineer, who had a deep interest in math and geometry. Pacioli and Leonardo became dear friends, and they began to collaborate on a number of large and important projects. Pacioli's famous work, *The Divine Proportion*, was illustrated by none other than Leonardo. That manuscript studied the geo-metric concept which Leonardo called "the Golden Proportion," a ratio of length to width which is approximately 1.618 to 1. Euclid wrote on this number — which modern mathematicians call phi — several hundred years before Christ. Even before Euclid addressed the higher math behind phi, the ancient Greeks and Egyptians considered the ratio visually appealing.

Before these Renaissance forefathers of the modern mili-tary-industrial complex could become too comfortable in their sinecures at Milan, Louis XII became king of France in 1498 and claimed the duchy of Milan for himself. The city-state of Venice threw in its lot with King Louis and allowed the French armies to take control of its ancient rivals in Milan. Ludovico Sforza was captured while trying to retake the city, and the court intellectuals fled for their lives. Leonardo returned to Florence. Unfortunately, French archers used Leonardo's great statue of Sforza's father as a target — and it was eventually destroyed by flight after flight of French arrows.

In 1502, Leonardo was hired by Cesare Borgia, Duke of Romagna, to continue creating machines of war. Not only a member of the infamous Borgia clan, he was also the son of Pope Alexander VI, who controlled a vast swath of Italian soil "in trust" for the Roman Catholic Church. Cesare hired Leonardo to build fortifications and a variety of military works projects. It was a time of artillery, not of art, so Leonardo spent little time in the studio. He did serve on the committee which decided where to place Michelangelo's famous statue of David, and he also began work on a mural for the Palazzo Vecchio. But like so much of Leonardo's artwork, the mural was never completed. Indeed, his only surviving painting from this period is the *Mona Lisa*.

In 1506, Leonardo returned to Milan. The city-state was still under French control, with Louis XII in residence. Leonardo became the Valois king's court painter, but again it appears that he finished little in the way of art — so much for Dan Brown's claim that Leonardo's "enormous output" funded his "lavish lifestyle." For of the works which have survived, only *The Virgin and Child with St. Anne* was completed during this period. Leonardo continued with his engineering commissions and also designed an equestrian figure for a proposed monument to the commander of the French forces in Milan. But it too was never completed. From 1514 to 1516 Leonardo lived in Rome, where he primarily focused on scientific studies in the court of Pope Leo X. He then moved to France, where King Francis I set him up at the Château de Cloux, near the royal summer palace at Amboise. Leonardo died there in 1519.

Enormous Output of Artwork?

Leonardo is regarded today not only as an artistic genius, but as a prodigy in such diverse fields as engineering, architecture, anatomy, physics, meteorology, geology, botany, and hydraulics. Two of his paintings, the *Mona Lisa* and *The Last Supper*, are among the most famous images in the world, and both are featured in *The Da Vinci Code*. Leonardo is a fascinating and enigmatic figure — indeed, the man himself is a yet undeciphered code.

As regards his artwork, Dan Brown is quite correct in calling it "breathtaking." Similarly, much of it is indeed Christian religious art. This makes sense because Europe in the late middle ages and early modern period was still vastly fractured by differences of language, regionalism, and complicated political allegiances. *The* unifying institution in western Europe was the Roman Catholic Church, whose influence across many feudal borders is seen in the lingua franca of religious iconography. Therefore Christian themes were standard fare in Renaissance fine arts.

But although Leonardo's work was breathtaking and his themes religious, his output was hardly as enormous as *The Da Vinci Code* claims. It is simply not true that his "vast number of lucrative Vatican commissions" funded his lavish lifestyle. On the contrary, Leonardo did remarkably few paintings or sculptures, and many of those were left *unfinished* — such as his first commission, an altarpiece for the town hall in Florence. His first large painting from 1481, *The Adoration of the Magi*, was never completed, nor were his paintings of *Saint Jerome* and *Saint John the Baptist*. These were not commissioned by the Vatican, either. Including incomplete works, his entire production of paintings is not much more than twenty, and of that number only a dozen survive. As far as we know, there was only one commission for the Vatican, and that remained unexecuted. On his death bed, Leonardo is supposed to have said that he regretted wasting so much of his life on science and having spent so little time on his painting. Perhaps it would be more truthful to say that Leonardo financed his flamboyant lifestyle by designing engines of war for the Dukes of Milan and Romagna — but it is patently untrue that he lived lavishly because of any "vast output of Christian art."

A Flamboyant Homosexual?

There is not a great deal of support for Brown's historically flip-
pant statement that Leonardo was a "flamboyant homosexual."
Early in his career, in 1476, Leonardo and four other artists
were anonymously accused of sodomy with Jacopo Salterelli,
an artist's model. The charge against the men was left mysteri-
ously in a public letter box at Florence's Palazzo Vecchio.
However, upon investigation all were acquitted of the charge
for lack of evidence. This one event represents the lone piece
of historical evidence for the claim that Leonardo was a homosexual.

Over four hundred years later, a second charge would be
deposited in the public square of academic opinion, although
its originator was far from anonymous. The great Viennese psychiatrist Sigmund Freud wrote in a book on the subject that
Leonardo may have been homosexual. Freud psychoanalyzed
the long-dead artist, using as his data an account of a child-
hood dream that Leonardo had written about. In the dream, a
bird comes to Leonardo while he is in his cradle. Based on his
translation of Leonardo's writing, Freud understood the bird to
be a vulture. In Leonardo's day it was popularly believed that
all vultures were, in fact, females capable of self-impregnation.
To Freud, the vulture would have served as a dream symbol of
mothers. Therefore according to Freud's version of Leonardo's
dream, the bird forcibly inserts its tail into the mouth of the
infant Leonardo. Freud believed that this represented both the
insertion of the mother's nipple and the insertion of a penis,
leading to sexual confusion and eventually homosexuality. As
it turns out, Freud's translation may have been an error; other

translators substitute "hawk" for "vulture" — hardly a female symbol.

While Freud's *ex post facto* analysis seems to be a stretch to me, it is a popular theory among some contemporary students of the puzzle that is Leonardo. A prominent London psychiatrist and the author of innumerable journal articles, Dr. Raj Persaud explains that Freud's theories are popular with many students of Leonardo because they seem to answer troubling aspects of Leonardo's career and work. Dr. Persaud believes that the bird dream is a fusion of several fantasies: a mother's passionate love (*the bird kissing him*), a boy's phallic image of his mother (*the bird's tail*), and his homosexual revision of both (*his sucking on the tail*). Freud felt that this dream solved a real Leonardo code, which is the encrypted inner life of the artist. Freud argued that the dream shows that Leonardo transformed his sexuality into an urge for knowledge, but from then on was unable to finish anything. Dr. Persaud argues that Leonardo's art supports Freud's thesis. For example, Leonardo's two paintings of John the Baptist suggest a degree of bisexuality in that they depict apparently androgynous males. Similarly, his drawings display a surprising ignorance of female genitals or any apparent knowledge of how heterosexual intercourse is usually performed.

The contemporary claim that the *Mona Lisa* is a disguised portrait of Leonardo in women's clothing is also upheld by Dr. Persaud. He argues that a comparison of the painting with a self-portrait of Leonardo shows that the facial features align exactly, as though Leonardo had painted his most famous work while looking at himself in the mirror. Leonardo kept the *Mona Lisa* with him until his death. If this was indeed a disguised self-portrait of the artist, Dr. Persaud thinks Leonardo's attachment to it would support Freud's hypothesis that Leonardo was a highly narcissistic homosexual.

So is it true? That Leonardo may have formed homosexual attachments is an interesting speculation, and it may offer a key to understanding the puzzle that is Leonardo. Nonetheless, while he might have been attracted to members of his own sex, the evidence from modern psychiatry is no more than educated guesswork. What is historically certain, however, is that Leonardo was no "flamboyant homosexual," as The Da Vinci Code claims. If he had been openly gay, much less flamboyant about it, it is likely that there would be some record of it beyond a single anonymous accusation. Moreover, it would be more likely that Leonardo might have decided to remain quietly in the closet after the public accusation of sodomy with Jacopo Salterelli.

The Woman at the Last Supper?

Leonardo is central to the thesis of The Da Vinci Code because the book assumes that he left a crucial clue about the nature of Jesus in his great painting, The Last Supper. This work depicts Jesus' last meal with his disciples before his arrest, trial, and execution. That event is, of course, central to Christian belief, and it is remembered in Christian churches at the celebration of the eucharist — also called the mass, or Holy Communion. The exact moment depicted in Leonardo's painting is the disciples' reaction to Jesus' statement, "One of you will betray me."

This same story is told in each of the four gospels with some variations. It appears from the painting itself that *The Last Supper* follows the narrative of the Gospel of John. The Gospel of John tells the story of the last supper this way:

> Jesus was troubled in spirit, and declared, "Very truly, I tell you, one of you will betray me." The disciples looked at one another, uncertain of whom he was speaking. One of the disciples — the one whom Jesus loved — was reclining next to him; Simon Peter therefore motioned to him to ask Jesus of whom he was speaking. So while reclining next to Jesus, he asked him, "Lord, who is it?" Jesus answered, "It is the one to whom I give this piece of bread when I have dipped it in the dish." So when he had dipped the piece of bread, he gave it to Judas son of Simon Iscariot. After he received the piece of bread, Satan entered into him. Jesus said to him, "Do quickly what you are going to do." (John 13: 21-27)

Leonardo painted *The Last Supper* in the mid-1490s on the dining room wall of the monastery of Santa Maria della Grazia in Milan. The mural is both an artistic triumph and a technical disaster: Leonardo used an experimental technique with this mural, mixing oil with paint in an attempt to slow the rate at which the paint dried. Unfortunately, this prevented the paint from being absorbed into the wall, and *The Last Supper* began to deteriorate almost immediately. Over the centuries, attempts have been made to restore the painting, with mixed success.

Still, the image is unforgettable. We see Jesus, in the center of the picture, seated behind a table. On his left are six figures, in two groups of three, standing or sitting behind the table, and on his right are six figures, also in two groups of three. Anyone familiar with the story would recognize immediately that this is Jesus and his twelve disciples.

A standard analysis of the painting emphasizes its highly geometrical and symmetrical composition and use of space. In his vision of the last supper event, Leonardo's is the first monumental depiction in fifteenth-century Italy to put Judas on the same side of the table as Christ and the other disciples; before this, Judas was shown sitting across from him. We see how each disciple reacts to Christ's announcement that one of them will betray him. To mark Judas as the betrayer, he is separated by a sudden thrust of a diagonal plane away from Christ.

Perhaps following the lessons in geometry he learned from Pacioli at the Sforza court, Leonardo uses a geometrical arrangement to emphasize the pathos of the disciples and the drama of the scene. First, we see how the four rectangular tapestries in the background divide the disciples into groups of three, each discussing Christ's shocking prediction of his coming betrayal. Second, Christ, with his arms outstretched, forms a triangle. This is more than merely a geometric allusion to the grouping of the disciples into three and the three windows on the back wall, for this three-sided shape is a symbol of the Holy Trinity. Third, the round arch above the central rear window forms a symbolic halo over Christ's head. This arch is a second reference to his sharing in the divine life of God as a member of the Holy Trinity, equal with the Father and the Spirit. It is part of the triune nature of the Godhead, as believed by Christians and important above all to the Gospel of John with its crystal clear statement of the equality of Jesus Christ with

God. Finally, the geometrical perspective of the painting draws the viewer's eye toward Christ at the center of the composition. All the painting's orthogonal lines (imaginary lines which run perpendicular to the plane of the picture) point to Christ. By this arrangement, Leonardo controls the observer's vision and directs it toward the figure of Christ. Jesus stretches his arms and hands forward so that as we observers are drawn in by the geometric construction of the painting's perspective, we are at the same time received by the outstretched arms of Christ.

Contrary to standard analysis, *The Da Vinci Code* offers a novel insight about the painting by questioning the sex of the person seated at Jesus' immediate right. The figure's "red hair," "delicate folded hands," and "hint of a bosom," seem to indicate that this person must be "without a doubt . . . female" (*Da Vinci Code*, 243). As *The Da Vinci Code* explains, the woman seated next to Jesus is Mary Magdalene.

We have to wonder why no one noticed this for five centuries. *The Da Vinci Code* explains it this way: "Our preconceived notions of this scene are so powerful that our mind blocks out the incongruity and overrides our eyes." *The Da Vinci Code* tells us also that grime and clumsy restorations obscured the details of the painting until it was restored in 1954. Or perhaps — no one noticed because it is the figure of a man, not a woman.

Chicago Art Institute curator Bruce Boucher explains that Leonardo's composition mostly "conforms to traditional Florentine depictions of the Last Supper." He explains further that at that time, "St. John was invariably represented as a beautiful young man whose special affinity with Jesus was expressed by his being seated at Jesus' right. Leonardo's figure of St. John conforms to this type."[1]

A couple of generations after Leonardo painted his famous version of the Last Supper, another prominent Italian, Paolo Veronese, painted a number of his own renditions of the Last Supper. A prominent representative of the Venetian school, Veronese added a number of features to his own paintings that the Roman Catholic hierarchy found highly objectionable — most notably, dogs and Germans. This was too much. So Veronese was summoned to a religious tribunal for questioning — what did his painting mean? Critic Jacques Barzun recounts a hilarious conversation between the artist and the Roman Catholic thought-police of the early sixteenth century:

> Church: *Do you know why you have been summoned?*
>
> Veronese: I can well imagine. Your Lordships had
>   ordered the Prior of the Convent to have a
>   Magdalene painted in the picture [of the
>   Lord's Last Supper] instead of the dog [I
>   painted there]. I told him that I would do
>   anything for my honor and that of the paint-
>   ing, but that I did not see how a figure of
>   Magdalene would be suitable there.
>
> Church: *Have you painted other Suppers besides this one?*
>
> Veronese: Yes, my lords. [He mentions five.]

It would seem that if the Roman Catholic church were requesting "Magdalenes" be inserted *into* depictions of the Last Supper, this would undermine *The Da Vinci Code*'s assertion that Leonardo did it surreptitiously. It would appear from this dialogue that even a relatively satirical church critic like Veronese saw that the Magdalene had no place in a depiction of the Last Supper.[2]

The Gospel of John calls the young John the "disciple whom Jesus loved." He is mentioned several times in the Gospel of John, where he is seated next to Jesus at the Last Supper. The Beloved Disciple, as he is traditionally called, also stood with Mary, the Mother of Jesus, at the foot of the cross. He ran with Peter to the tomb after Mary Magdalene told them it was empty, and he was the first to believe that Jesus had risen. John was the first to recognize the resurrected Jesus in Galilee, and he heard Jesus contrast his own fate with that of Peter at the very end of the gospel. Ancient Christian tradition, dating from the late first century, holds that the Beloved Disciple was John, the son of Zebedee, the apostolic figure whose teaching is traditionally part of the Gospel of John.

Tradition also has it that John was the youngest of the original twelve disciples, and therefore, as Boucher explains in his article, medieval and later artists adopted the Christian iconographic convention of portraying the Beloved Disciple as a lovely youth. So it is to be *expected* from religious artistic conventions in Leonardo's day that the figure on Jesus' right in *The Last Supper* would be beardless and look slightly effeminate. To fifteenth-century artists and viewers of art, the effeminate, beardless youth *was* the way John the Beloved Disciple was to be painted. And there are numerous examples to prove it. In a thirteenth-century icon from the Kress collection, John has light red hair, no beard, smooth ivory skin, and inclines his head in a way that is almost seductive. In an illuminated

French manuscript dating from the 1420s, owned by the National Gallery in Washington, D.C., John is depicted at work on his gospel with no beard and a delicate, feminine expression. In Florentine painter Civerchio's 1502 painting of Christ, Peter, and John, the latter has a smooth white face, reddish locks, and dewy-eyed expression.

There is nothing about *The Last Supper* which is surprising or unconventional other than the location of the figure of Judas on the same side of the table as Jesus. What is surprising, but never mentioned in *The Da Vinci Code*, is the way Leonardo depicts another John — John the Baptist — in two of his last paintings. Both of these show him looking decidedly feminine. Traditionally John the Baptist was a rugged, bearded, and often older man, preaching in the wilderness, wearing animal skins, and eating locusts. So there was very little precedent for Leonardo's rendition of the Baptist. Presumably Leonardo had his reasons, but regardless, if Leonardo could paint an effeminate John the Baptist *against* iconographic norms, he could certainly paint an effeminate John the Beloved Disciple in accordance with those conventions.

When I look at *The Last Supper* I don't see a woman sitting next to Jesus. What I see is a moment in time from the gospel of John. Jesus tells his disciples that one of them will betray him. The disciples look at one another, uncertain of whom he is speaking. One of the disciples, the one whom Jesus loved, is reclining next to him. Peter motions to him to ask Jesus of whom he is speaking. This is what the mural portrays. Yes, Leonardo gives us a breathtakingly beautiful religious mural laden with geometrical and theological encoding, but those "codes" serve as artistic and symbolic tools — not to hide a secret, but to bring life and meaning to a scene well-known from the life of Christ.

The facts of Leonardo's life are fascinating, and the fact that he did paint so few works, spent much of his career in the military service of dukes, and left so much work unfinished is curious. As Freud wrote four centuries after Leonardo's lifetime, the artist was an enigmatic puzzle of a man. Whether he was a homosexual is an unknowable fact — unless and until better evidence is uncovered. Certainly, the psychoanalysis of Sigmund Freud and Dr. Raj Persaud is fascinating and perhaps correct, but hardly conclusive. Episcopal priest and art historian Susan Barnes says quite simply, "There are no solid historical grounds whatsoever to claim that Leonardo was a 'flamboyant homosexual.'" Despite *The Da Vinci Code's* statements, furthermore, we know that Leonardo painted relatively little, and never for the Vatican. And while *The Last Supper* does include geometric and iconographic codes, these are used to further the expression of a well-known biblical scene.

CHAPTER THREE

Constantine, Jesus, and the Bible

Constantine needed to strengthen the new Christian tradition, and held a famous ecumenical gathering known as the Council of Nicaea....Many aspects of Christianity were debated and voted upon — the date of Easter, the role of bishops, the administration of sacraments, and, of course, the *divinity* of Jesus....Until that moment in history, Jesus was viewed by His followers as a mortal prophet...a great and powerful man, but a *man* nonetheless....Jesus' establishment as the "Son of God" was officially proposed and voted on by the Council of Nicaea...Jesus' divinity was the result of a *vote*...a relatively close vote at that. (*Da Vinci Code*, 233)

For the first half of the book, *The Da Vinci Code* is a truly entertaining murder mystery. As I read it I was swept away by the plot and its intriguing puzzles. Indeed, there is nothing in the first half of the book that should make me, or any other

Christian, bristle. Of course there are plenty of inaccuracies and distortions in this first half that we have already explored, but as I read on it was easy to suspend my disbelief about those matters because the story had fully grabbed my attention. I found the first half of The Da Vinci Code interesting, clever, and enjoyable.

About halfway through, however, the novel changed, and it became impossible for me to suspend my disbelief any longer. Instead of continuing to play loosely with the facts simply for the sake of the story, all of a sudden The Da Vinci Code seems to switch from murder mystery to anti-Christian rant. I don't mean that The Da Vinci Code drops the murder mystery entirely, but the book seems more interested in preaching its views on Christianity than in merely telling a tall tale. The author begins to adopt a pretense of scholarship and factuality as he asserts that the central doctrines of Christianity are the result of an ingenious fraud on the part of the Emperor Constantine to secure the support of the up-and-coming Christian faction in the Empire. Before Constantine, we are told, Christians all thought that Jesus was merely a man and a prophet. As a kind of imperial power play, therefore, Constantine engineered a vote at the Council of Nicaea to declare Jesus the divine Son of God and arranged to incorporate pagan concepts into a bastardized form of Jesus' original teachings. Thus the book claims that the Emperor stole Jesus from his original followers, hijacked his humanist message, and shrouded those teachings in an impenetrable cloak of divinity to expand his own imperial power. It tells us that "because Constantine upgraded Jesus' status almost four centuries after Jesus' death," Constantine had to create a "new Bible, which omitted those gospels that spoke of Christ's human traits and embellished those gospels that made him godlike. The earlier gospels were outlawed, gathered up, and burned." The book argues "that almost everything our fathers taught us about Christ is false" (*Da Vinci Code*, 234-5).

To me, as a Christian, *The Da Vinci Code*'s claims about Constantine and the formation of Christian doctrine are bizarre and horrifying, especially since many people now believe they are true.

Fortunately, if we take the time to explore the history behind such claims, it will become clear that they are not only *spiritually* but also *factually* untrue. The history of the formation of Christian doctrine is well documented, as is the role of the Emperor Constantine in that history. Whether or not we subscribe to the Christian faith itself, the general *history* of that faith is widely agreed upon — and that history bears almost no relationship to *The Da Vinci Code*'s version. The book is correct in arguing that Constantine was a giant in church history and a force to be reckoned with. But it is vastly incorrect in claiming he had comparable influence on the church's most essential doctrines — like the divinity of Christ or the shape of the Bible!

The truth is that Constantine's influence on the church was more historical and institutional than theological. Indeed, he did call for the first great council of the church to discuss both *essential* theological matters, such as the divinity of Christ, and *inessential* organizational issues, such as fixing the date of Easter, the role of bishops, and the division of Christian churches into provinces. But the Council of Nicaea was not a contentious corporate annual meeting where the CEO imposes a corrupt agenda on his hapless shareholders. What happened at Nicaea was the first-ever massive, ecumenical public gathering of Christians from all over the world, both eastern and western Christendom. Vastly diverse human beings, united by faith in Christ, came together to talk about their beliefs and settle their differences with no fear of imperial violence against them.

The Da Vinci Code is certainly correct that Constantine presided over that first universal meeting of Christian minds with imperial pride and honor, but he most certainly did not force any semi-pagan theology down the bishops' throats. Instead, his council reaffirmed Christian orthodoxy by saying that Jesus was fully human and fully God, over against the followers of a teacher and theologian called Arius who did not believe in the full divinity of the Christ. The proof of this is in the very creed itself. The language of the creed that came out of Nicaea, which Christians still recite at every Holy Eucharist, tracks very well with the language of the New Testament. Moreover, it follows the teachings articulated further by the great "Fathers" of the church, theologians like Origen and Irenaeus who lived in the second and third centuries of the Christian era. Although the confession of faith called the Nicene Creed dates to the fourth century and not the first, it is most certainly biblical and apostolic in nature. We know this because the apostles left us their beliefs in the books and letters that became the New Testament.

As for the books that make up the New Testament, far from being "produced" by Constantine in the fourth century, they had been written down and collected together by the end of the first century. The first compilation of these books —

what is called the "canon of the New Testament" — was circulated in the middle of the second century, and was generally adopted within another lifetime. Since all kinds of Christian writing and gospels were circulating orally in the years after Jesus' resurrection, it was important for the church to adopt a "canon," literally, "rule," that confirmed which writings were going to be adopted as the standard of authentic teaching for Christians.

The only biblical books to be debated after the second century were relatively minor books of the New Testament canon, such as the letters from James and Jude. These disputed texts saw their apostolic authenticity disputed here and there for a long time — even Martin Luther disliked James, Jude, and Revelation. But while the New Testament canon may not have always had precisely twenty-seven books, at least the four gospels and the letters of Paul, John, Peter, and their followers were considered "biblical" since the late first century and early second. On the other hand, the so-called "gnostic gospels," which have made their way into the popular imagination through the writings of New Testament scholar Elaine Pagels, were never universally accepted. And even they were written and largely discarded *before* Constantine's day.

So Constantine had little to do with the formation of Christian doctrine, although he did call the Council of Nicaea and used his imperial power to give its decisions the power of law. A highly readable academic text on the formation of the ancient Christian creeds is Frances Young's *The Making of the Creeds*. Professor Young's book is pertinent to this discussion because it mentions Constantine only three times — and in no instance does he have anything to do with the formation of the

Nicene or any other creed. All she says about Constantine was that his influence on the *institutional* hierarchy ended up leading to the strengthening of Christian monasticism.

So who was Constantine, and what did he really do?

A Short Sketch of Constantine the Great

Flavius Valerius Constantinus was born in what is now Serbia in the early 270s. His father, Constantius, was a Roman general, and his mother, Helena, was a woman of low social standing ("a stable girl," or *stabularia*, according to Ambrose of Milan in 395). In 306, Constantius became ruler of the empire's western provinces, but he did not hold office long. The next year he was killed in Britain, fighting the Picts of what is now Scotland. Constantine had accompanied his father to York in the north of England, and there, after his father's death, the troops proclaimed Constantine their emperor. The Roman Senate and Praetorian Guard, however, endorsed Maxentius, the son of a former Emperor — and Constantine's brother-in-law. The two rivals maintained an uneasy truce for several years, but then civil war erupted between them. At the Battle of Milvian Bridge in October of 312, Constantine defeated Maxentius and became sole emperor in the West.

The night before the battle, Constantine is supposed to have received a divine message. According to one report, he was told in a dream to put the sign of Christ on his soldiers' shields. Another story claims that the whole army saw a cross of light in the sky, in broad daylight, and the words "by this sign you will be victor." Whatever the metaphysical details of the story may in fact be, Constantine won the battle and credited the victory to the Christian God.

For Christians, this turned out to be extremely good news. Until Constantine's ascendancy to power, since the time of Nero in the first century, thousands of Christians were persecuted, tortured, and killed for their faith. There were numerous waves of imperial oppression of both Christians and Jews. We have some records of the persecutions these followers of Jesus suffered at the hand of the Romans; for example, the historian Suetonius wrote approvingly of Nero's punishment of the Christians, "a set of men adhering to a novel and mischievous superstition." His contemporary Pliny the Younger explained to the Emperor Trajan how he had handled the Christian problem in Bithynia. When persons accused of Christianity were brought before him, he asked them three times if they were Christians, and if they admitted it and refused to recant, he sentenced them to death. Pliny explained to the emperor that he did not really understand the nature of the crime of being a Christian, but "their pertinacity and inflexible obstinacy should certainly be punished." Even high-ranking Roman women would be killed if found out to be "unrepentant Christians." A famous example is the martyrdom of Perpetua and Felicity — an African aristocrat and her pregnant servant — who were Christians together and were executed by the state in 203 for their bold proclamation of faith in Jesus Christ. The great African bishop, Tertullian, spread their story throughout the church as a sign of their apostolic witness to Christ in death in the first decade of the third century.

Not all Christians had the courage of Perpetua and Felicity. Many, when faced with the choice of apostasy (*denying belief in Christ*) or death, chose apostasy. The brutal and terrifying conditions under which early Christians lived is clearly shown by the fact that one major dispute within the early church, the North African Donatist controversy, was over whether someone who had once apostasized in order to save his or her life should be permitted into the church ever afterward. The Donatists argued that such "cowards" should be forbidden from church membership. Others took a more merciful approach. Ultimately the party of mercy and flexibility prevailed, while the hard-liners became a schismatic branch of the church.

During the reign of Diocletian, a few years before Constantine donned the imperial purple in 324, thousands of Christians were tortured and put to death in the Great Persecution for refusing to adhere to the imperial cult. One of Constantine's first official acts, several years before Milvian Bridge, was to end all such persecution in the area he controlled. After Milvian Bridge, he and his co-emperor, the Emperor of the East, Licinius, issued the Edict of Milan, which promised religious freedom for Christians and "all others." As time went on, Constantine provided increasing support to the Christian church. Although he did not establish Christianity as the official church of the Roman Empire, he favored it over other religions.

Why did Constantine favor Christianity? Brown's answer, through the character of Leigh Teabing, is that "Constantine was a very good businessman. He could see that Christianity was on the rise, and he simply backed the winning horse" (*Da*

Vinci Code, 232). This might be true in a sense. After all, Constantine was not a business man, but he certainly was a politician. And when we seek to know the motivations for a politician's actions, our first answer is generally "political self-interest." Maybe this was a key issue for Constantine — indeed, I'm sure it was. But, what is unclear is how it was possible that he saw Christianity as any kind of "winning horse"? Indeed, before Constantine halted the Great Persecution, Christianity probably looked to him more like a horse headed for the glue factory than the winner's circle. Christianity was only a "winning horse" after the crucial protection and financial support of Constantine and his pious and influential mother, not before. Most students of Constantine argue that while we will never fully understand his true inner motivations, it appears from the record that his mother's faith was hugely influential on her son. Since the time of St. Ambrose, Christians have viewed Helena as a humble "stable girl," whose own Christian faith softened and influenced both her lover Constantius and her son Constantine.

Just how softened Constantine was by his Christian beliefs is often hard to see from the facts of his life. After all, he became the sole emperor by defeating and executing both Licinius and Licinius' son. Two years later, after a horrible series of plots, accusations, and various palace intrigues between his second wife and his eldest son, the emperor executed his own son, Crispus, and his second wife Fausta, the mother of his three younger sons. It has long been believed that this series of events led to his mother Helena's pilgrimage to Jerusalem in 326 — she went as an act of penance for her son's bloody actions.

With Constantine's political supremacy assured, the emperor consolidated the empire by uniting East and West into one and founded Constantinople. That great new city would be the New Rome, and it was built on the site of the ancient Greek Byzantium. The new capital, dedicated in 330, had none of the pagan monuments and shrines of the first Rome. Constantinople would be a city of churches, including Hagia Sophia (*Holy Wisdom*), Hagia Eirene (*Holy Peace*), and the Church of the Holy Apostles, all commissioned by Constantine and funded from the imperial treasury.

In 337, Constantine fell ill. He traveled to Nicomedia, where he was baptized and, a few weeks later, died. His body was returned to Constantinople and placed in the Church of the Holy Apostles, in accordance with his wishes, making him-self — symbolically, at least — one of the apostles.

Constantine's personal religious beliefs remain somewhat mysterious. *The Da Vinci Code* describes Constantine as "a life-long pagan who was baptized on his deathbed, too weak to protest" (*Da Vinci Code*, 232). It is certainly true that early in his reign, before the battle at the Milvian Bridge, Constantine worshiped Apollo, reverenced as Sol Invictus, or "the Unconquered Sun." It is also a fact that he was not baptized a Christian until he was near death — but it is a fallacy to say that he was baptized against his will. Moreover, what we would call the "lateness" of his baptism does not imply that Constantine did not embrace the tenets of Christianity well before his death.

Indeed, it was common at this time to postpone baptism to the end of one's life, especially if one's duty as an official included torture and execution of criminals. Baptism, with its washing away of sins, was and is a once-in-a-lifetime cleansing. It was believed in the early centuries of the church that if one's profession required one to sin (like a warrior or Roman authority), it was prudent to put off baptism until late age or severe illness made further sin unlikely and judgment imminent. A. H. M. Jones writes in his book *The Later Roman Empire* that the emperors Constantius II and Theodosius I, as well as St. Ambrose, were among those who delayed baptism until late in life. Indeed St. Ambrose, who had grown up in Trier in the shadow of Helena Augusta's regional palace, was not baptized until *after* he was elected bishop! Although certainly a believer, Ambrose like many others put off baptism because of the great fear of what was called post-baptismal sin.

Whatever may have been Constantine's personal beliefs, he did express a number of Christian ideals in a variety of his public actions. Notably, Constantine assigned a fixed proportion of imperial revenue to fund church charities, and he passed laws which offered new protections to children, slaves, peasants, and prisoners. He even prohibited the facial branding of criminals because of the belief that men and women were made in the image and likeness of God.

Who Wrote the Bible?

The Da Vinci Code explains that the "fundamental irony of Christianity" is that the Bible "was collated by the pagan Roman Emperor Constantine the Great" (*Da Vinci Code*, 231). As I have said before, the Bible was preserved in written texts and "collated" centuries before Constantine was born. It is rather unclear what *The Da Vinci Code* means by "the Bible," but one must assume he means the Christian Bible, which consists of the Old and New Testaments.

The Hebrew scriptures were completed seven to eight centuries before Constantine's time, and some of them are much older than that. Most scholars believe that the books of the Law were finalized some time before the fifth century BCE, while the books of the Prophets and the Writings took their final form sometime before 250. At that time the Hebrew scriptures were translated into Greek — a volume called the "Septuagint," Greek for "seventy," after the seventy translators — for the benefit of Jews living in Alexandria and other Greek-speaking cities. A number of other holy books were composed by these pious Greek-speaking Jews, furthermore, and they would comprise what is now called the Apocrypha.

In 90 CE at the Council of Jamnia, a group of Jewish rabbis reached agreement on which scriptures would be considered part of the "canon" (that is, which were sacred or authoritative), and they standardized the texts of those scriptures. As a result of the rabbis' declaration that the Hebrew scriptures were a "closed canon," Christian scriptures could not become part of the Jewish canon, and Jewish Christians were expelled from the synagogues. Christians, however, would make the Jewish canon part of their Bible. We possess plenty of ancient manuscripts to prove that Constantine had nothing to do with the creation of the Old Testament. The Dead Sea Scrolls have no New Testament books at all — although they do contain fragments of all the books of the Old Testament — and these scrolls were all composed long before Constantine's day.

As to the New Testament, most scholars agree that the twenty-seven books of the New Testament were written down before the end of the first century. Likewise, most scholars agree that the gospels of Matthew, Mark, and Luke, and all of Paul's letters, were in widespread circulation among Christian communities before the rabbinical council expelled Christians from Judaism in 90 CE By the middle of second century the leading bishops of Europe, Africa, and Asia recognized a basic core of the New Testament canon — four gospels and about a dozen apostolic letters. The selection process was fairly complex: each book of the Bible had to be written or sponsored by an apostle, orthodox in content, and publicly in use by a number of churches. This discernment process went on in the West until 397, after Constantine's death, when the canon was finally fixed.

Is Christianity Based on Paganism?

The Da Vinci Code claims that nothing in Christianity is original, and credits Constantine with creating a new religion by fusing pagan symbols, dates, and rituals into the evolving Christian tradition.

Now, it is neither inaccurate nor particularly startling to claim that Christianity has incorporated pagan symbols and practices into itself. You need only think of Christmas trees, Easter bunnies, and the cross itself to know that — the cross is an ancient pagan instrument of execution. But the fact that pagan symbols have been grafted onto Christianity does not mean that Christianity was "created" through a "fusion" with paganism, and it certainly it doesn't mean that Constantine did the fusing.

Historically Christianity is based on Judaism. Jesus was a Jew, and all of his disciples were Jews. The God that they worshipped was the God of Abraham and Isaac and Jacob, the God of Moses and Elijah, the God of Jesus' ancestor King David. Throughout the gospels, Jesus refers again and again to the Hebrew scriptures, and so does Paul in his letters to the young churches. Sometimes Jesus cites the Hebrew scriptures as authorities to prove a point. For example, when the Pharisees complained that the disciples were violating the sabbath by plucking grain to eat, Jesus reminded them of the story of David feeding his companions on sacramental bread from the high priest's altar. "The sabbath was made for humankind, and not humankind for the sabbath," Jesus concluded from this example.[1] At other times, Jesus used the Hebrew scriptures as a jumping off point for a lesson that went in a different direction. The famous parable of the Good Samaritan is a commentary (or *midrash*) on the Hebrew injunction to "love your neighbor as yourself." Jesus told the story to ask the question, "Who is your neighbor?"[2]

As good Jews, Jesus and his followers did not look to paganism as a source of religious insight. They were confident that the pagans had it all wrong. There is a wonderful story in the book of Acts about the apostle Paul in Athens, distressed to see that it was a city of pagan idols. When given the chance to do so, he let the Athenian pagans know how mistaken they were.

So they took him and brought him to the Areopagus and asked him, "May we know what this new teaching is that you are presenting? It sounds rather strange to us, so we would like to know what it means." Now all the Athenians and the foreigners living there would spend their time in nothing but telling or hearing something new.

Then Paul stood in front of the Areopagus and said, "Athenians, I see how extremely religious you are in every way. For as I went through the city and looked carefully at the objects of your worship, I found among them an altar with the inscription, 'To an unknown god.' What therefore you worship as unknown, this I proclaim to you. The God who made the world and everything in it, he who is Lord of heaven and earth, does not live in shrines made by human hands, nor is he served by human hands, as though he needed anything, since he himself gives to all mortals life and breath and all things."[3]

Therefore *The Da Vinci Code* has it right when it claims that the underlying beliefs of Christianity were "nothing new." But it is wrong to claim they came from paganism or Constantine. They came from Judaism, and from there were incorporated into Christianity at its very beginning!

As the passage quoted above from Acts attests, when Christianity began to spread out from Judea into the wider world of the Roman Empire, it came into contact with a variety of pagan religions. Among these were the so-called "mystery" cults, such as Mithraism. Not a great deal is known about the details of these rites, because they were supposed to be secret to all but initiates. But they seem to have included eating the meat and drinking the blood of animal sacrifices, and they featured gods who periodically died and were reborn. Some have speculated that the mystery cults might have played a role in the development of the Christian sacraments of eucharist and baptism, and even the concept of resurrection.

But these suggestions have now largely been discredited. Even if such a connection between the mystery cults and Christianity existed, it would have been established by the middle of the first century, because by then baptism, eucharist, and the doctrine of Christ's resurrection were well established in the church. Paul's letters attest to this almost three hundred years before Constantine's father ever spent the night in the Bithynian stable where Helena was working and Constantine was conceived.

The most popular form of paganism in Constantine's day was solar monotheism. As mentioned above, Constantine worshiped the Unconquered Sun before his vision at the Milvian Bridge. It seems probable that Christians had an easier time converting monotheistic pagans than polytheistic ones. Indeed, the record shows that Christian concepts were frequently expressed in solar imagery long before Constantine's day. Theologian Clement of Alexandria spoke of Jesus Christ driving his chariot across the sky like the god of the sun. A well-known mosaic in Rome, probably created in the early fourth century, shows Christ as the sun god, mounting the heavens with his chariot. African bishop Tertullian, who was born in 160 CE, said that a great many of the pagans in his day thought Christians worshiped the sun because they met on Sundays and prayed toward the East.

Constantine did not invent any of this, nor was he responsible for Christian worship on Sunday. Robert Langdon, *The Da Vinci Code*'s Harvard iconographer, explains that Christians "originally observed the Jewish sabbath of Saturday" until Constantine changed it to "coincide with the pagan's veneration day of the sun" (*Da Vinci Code*, 232-3).

In fact, as historian Henry Chadwick points out, "the Christian practice of commemorating the Lord's resurrection on the first day of the week was already traditional before St. Paul wrote First Corinthians. The Church derived the habit of worship on one day in seven from Judaism, . . . and they chose Sunday as the day when the Lord rose again."[4] What Constantine did do, however, was to issue a decree in 321 that declared Sunday a day of rest. This was not a theological decree — it was the first Blue Law.

Who Was Jesus?

Character Leigh Teabing says that before the Council of Nicaea, "Jesus was viewed by his followers as a mortal prophet . . . a great and powerful man, but a man nonetheless. A mortal." He argues that Constantine changed this fundamental teaching and burnt all scriptures that said otherwise.

A moment's thought will show that this claim is impossible. If Christians in 325 had believed that Jesus was merely a man and a prophet, a vote by the bishops at Nicaea would not have changed their minds. And it certainly wouldn't have made them forget their earlier beliefs. Suppose that the history faculty at Harvard voted to declare that George Washington had been the first king of the United States, not the first president. Would you believe it? Would you forget that you had believed all your life that he was the first president?

Moreover, all scholars — even those who reject the religious claims of Christianity — agree that the early church firmly believed in the divinity of Jesus. Consider the letters of Paul and his circle of followers. Their apostolic authenticity is without question the best attested of all the Christian and Gnostic writings. They are clearly the oldest writings in the New Testament, dated by even the most liberal scholars to between 49-62 CE. Even Marcion, the great Gnostic theologian and teacher, revered Paul above all others. Paul's letters clearly state his understanding that Jesus was the Messiah, and of a stature equal to God. As he writes in Philippians from the year 50:

> Let the same mind be in you that was in Christ Jesus, who, though he was in the form of God, did not regard equality with God as something to be exploited, but emptied himself, taking the form of a slave, being born in human likeness. And being found in human form, he humbled himself and became obedient to the point of death — even death on a cross. Therefore God also highly exalted him and gave him the name that is above every name, so that at the name of Jesus every knee should bend, in heaven and on earth and under the earth, and every tongue should confess that Jesus Christ is Lord, to the glory of God the Father. (Philippians 2:5-11)

Paul portrays Jesus as both "in the form of God" and having been "born in human likeness." That seems paradoxical.

How could Jesus be both divine and human? In trying to avoid this paradox, some early followers of Jesus decided that the answer was that Jesus only *appeared* to be human. This idea was called "Docetism," from the Greek word for "to appear," and Gnostics generally agreed. At the other end of the spectrum were those who believed that Jesus was only human, and not divine at all. "Ebionites" were Jewish Christians who regarded Jesus as an ordinary human being who was overtaken by the power of God. Neither extreme, however, believed that Jesus *was* God.

We have a series of letters from a bishop called Ignatius of Antioch, in the very early second century, which refute both kinds of false teaching. Ignatius spoke with considerable authority. He had been sentenced to death by the Roman authorities for refusing to renounce Christianity, and these letters were written on his journey from Antioch to Rome, where he was to be thrown to the wild beasts in the Coliseum. In response to the Ebionites, Ignatius asserted that a merely human Jesus could not redeem humankind of its sins; only a divine sacrifice could do what Jesus claimed to do. His rejection of the Docetists was even more powerful: "If, as some godless men, that is, unbelievers, say, [Jesus] suffered in mere appearance, . . . why am I in bonds?"

Instead Ignatius espoused the paradoxical position that Jesus was both fully human and fully divine, "one person of two natures." Over the next two centuries, Christians thought — and fought and argued — about the full implications of this dual nature of Christ. But there was no substantial disagreement on the principle that Jesus was divine as well as human. So the position described by Leigh Teabing, that Jesus was "a mortal prophet . . . a great and powerful man, but a man nonetheless," was thoroughly discredited by theologians long before the time of Constantine.

The controversy that would be resolved at Nicaea was over the definition of Jesus' divinity and how he was related to God the Father. But to be clear, *both* sides of the debate believed Jesus was the Son of God. Nobody was saying at Nicaea, "Jesus is only a mortal prophet."

The so-called heretic in the debate was Arius, a Carthaginian Christian, who had studied in Antioch and was ordained to the clergy in Alexandria. He argued with Alexander, his bishop in Alexandria, over the exact nature of the Son of God. Arius taught that Jesus' true nature, even though divine, was somehow less so than the divinity of God the Father, although still superior to everybody else. Arius asserted that Jesus was the Messiah, and indeed, the Son of God, but he was still the "creation" of God. Therefore, although God had always existed, there was a time when the Son did not.

Athanasius was a brilliant young priest who took up the orthodox side in the debate. His point was that that the Logos, or the Word of God, the Son, was not created but rather "begotten" by God the Father. Like God, the Son had existed from all eternity as an equal partner of God and the Holy Spirit as one of the three persons of the Trinity. In other words, Athanasius argued that "there was no time before the Son existed"; Arius argued, "Yes there was — before the Son was created, he did not exist." In Greek, the difference came down to one letter: Athanasius said that the Son was of one and the same substance or being with the Father, or *homoousios*. Arius argued that the Son was "of like substance" with the Father, or *homoiousios*.

Now, for most of us, the one-letter difference between "homoousios" and "homoiousios" is still hard to understand. In his *Rise and Fall of the Roman Empire* historian Edward Gibbon scornfully observed that Christianity was split over a single *iota*! But all this aside, it is absolutely clear that the argument was never about whether or not Jesus was divine — that was a given for both sides.

What was also agreed on by both sides was the Bible. The followers of both Athanasius and Arius recognized the same exact collection of Holy Scripture — depending only on books from the recognized canon of the New Testament. Despite Dan Brown's assertion that Constantine's henchmen eliminated scores of Arian texts which emphasized only the human side of Jesus, both Arius and Athanasius were working from the same exact basis in Scripture. Both men thought they were "catholic," "orthodox," and "apostolic" in their beliefs; Arius felt he was well within the boundaries of established biblical tradition. What divided these two men was a highly sophisticated argument over the meaning of terminology and the interpretation of scripture, but they did argue from common scriptural grounds. This fact is highly significant because it shows that the essential shape of the Bible was recognized by all.

What Happened at Nicaea?

Constantine convened the Council of Nicaea in 325, with bishops in attendance from across the entire known world. It was the first *ecumenical* council (from the Greek word meaning "household.") It is not surprising that the first such meeting was held under Constantine. Until he came to power, persecution made it too risky for Christians to meet in the open and discuss their practices and beliefs in the public arena.

Such a council was the only way that disputes within the church could be resolved, because the church itself had no central authority. During the first five centuries of Christian history, no single Christian bishop could claim to speak for the entire church. Each bishop had authority only over his own diocese and region. The bishops (the direct descendants of the early "overseers" and "apostles") were in a relationship of brotherly equals with one another. The bishops of Jerusalem, Antioch, Alexandria, and Rome might enjoy particular prestige, but they had no power over other bishops. When Dan Brown refers to Nicaea as consolidating "the new Vatican power base" he is guilty of gross anachronism. In Constantine's day the bishop of Rome was just another bishop, not the leader of the whole Catholic Church, and the Vatican was still just a hill in Rome where Constantine was building a basilica over the grave of St. Peter.

The council was called primarily to resolve the Arian controversy, and Constantine was the presiding officer. There is no indication that Constantine cared one way or the other about Arianism, and it appears from his letters to the various parties involved that he felt they were in error only for bringing up such an ambiguous quibble over things largely unknowable to human minds. It appears further that Constantine just wanted the whole debate to go away and be settled. In that one goal, he failed.

Although the bishops did produce a working definition of the orthodox faith, the Nicene Creed itself was not finished until 381. There was a vote on the statement of faith at Nicaea, but it was far from "reasonably close" as *The Da Vinci Code* claims. Of the two hundred twenty bishops voting, all but two endorsed the creed and Arius himself was not allowed to vote, as he was not a bishop. The two dissenters were bishops from Libya, who apparently objected to a provision that put them under the control of the bishop of Alexandria. It appears that this near-unanimity was probably the result of misunderstandings over what the words of the draft creed actually meant, since the dispute went on until the eleventh century.[5] So as much as Constantine wanted things settled, his council did nothing to end theological controversy in the church even under a strong Christianizing emperor. The controversies of Nicaea — between Arians and Orthodox — continued for most of the fourth century. There were many followers of Arius in the Greek and Gothic parts of the Empire — including Constantine's own mother. When Constantine was baptized at the end of his life, the sacrament was performed by Eusebius, the Arian bishop of Nicomedia.

What Didn't Happen at Nicaea

Dan Brown's book tells Christians that their religion is based on a fraud and that they have been duped by a fourth-century pagan's political power play. That is simply wrong. Constantine did not "invent" Christianity by deifying a human prophet and then combining the worship of this new deity with bits and pieces of pagan sun worship. Nor did Constantine create a new Christian Bible by burning the gospels that told the truth about Jesus. The essentials of Christianity had been established for centuries before the time of Constantine. So were the Christian scriptures. The divine nature of Jesus was a central part of Christian belief from the beginning. No one at Nicaea disputed it.

CHAPTER FOUR

Gnosticism and the Lost Gospels

Teabing said, going to a nearby table of books, "As I said earlier, the marriage of Jesus and Mary Magdalene is part of the historical record." He began pawing through his book collection.... Teabing located a huge book and pulled it toward him across the table. The leather-bound edition was poster-sized, like a huge atlas. The cover read: *The Gnostic Gospels*.... "These are photocopies of the Nag Hammadi and Dead Sea scrolls, which I mentioned earlier," Teabing said. "The earliest Christian records. Troublingly, they do not match up with the gospels in the Bible." (*Da Vinci Code*, 245-6)

To prove its claim that Mary Magdalene was the wife of Jesus and the mother of his children, *The Da Vinci Code* is not content to rely only on secret messages in Renaissance paintings. It also argues that their marriage is part of the "historical record" found in two short and controversial passages

from Gnostic texts, which the character Leigh Teabing erroneously calls the "earliest Christian records."

This question of the "historical record" of a marriage
between Jesus and Mary Magdalene ties in with Brown's fantasy that Constantine invented a new Christian religion in the
fourth century by turning a mortal Jesus into a divine Christ.
Supposedly Constantine transformed Jesus' status from mortal
to divine four centuries after the crucifixion, when "thousands
of documents already existed chronicling His life as a *mortal
man.*" Therefore the emperor ordered that these earlier
"gospels," which portrayed Jesus as a wholly mortal human
prophet and not divine, be "outlawed, gathered up, and
burned" (*Da Vinci Code*, 234). Some of these gospels, Brown
tells us, were rediscovered in the mid-twentieth century among
the Dead Sea Scrolls in Palestine and in a cache of "Coptic
scrolls" found in Egypt. *The Da Vinci Code* cites passages from
two of these "Gnostic gospels," the Gospel of Philip and the
Gospel of Mary, which purport to prove that Jesus and Mary
were married.

What is the story behind these secret gospels, and who are
the Gnostics? Again, some of these claims are truthful and
some are completely false. The truth is that the Gnostics did
exist, and they competed with orthodox Christianity during its
first several centuries, writing "gospels" and other texts setting
out their religious beliefs. It is also true that dozens of ancient
texts were indeed discovered in the twentieth century in
Palestine and Egypt. These two major discoveries are among
the most important for biblical scholarship in the past fifty
years, shedding new light on our traditional understanding of
Christianity and Judaism. Although the newly discovered texts

were not all "Gnostic," the Gnostic texts among them have attracted particular attention because so little Gnostic writing was known before this.

Many religion scholars today are talking about them. Elaine Pagels is probably the most well-known American scholar of the Gnostics, and her book, *The Gnostic Gospels*, is one of the most popular books on the subject. She offers valuable insights into what the Gnostics may have been all about, and it would appear that Dan Brown draws some of his conclusions from Dr. Pagels' work. The problem with *The Da Vinci Code*'s treatment of Gnosticism and these textual discoveries is that once again the book distorts the facts and makes unsubstantiated claims.

Read objectively, none of these newly-discovered texts includes any "historical record" of a marriage between Jesus and Mary Magdalene. For those of us interested in the serious implications of these rediscovered ancient religious texts, we need to get our facts straight, and *The Da Vinci Code* won't help us there. We need to go beyond *The Da Vinci Code* to take a look at the Gnostics and the gospels they produced.

What Is Gnosticism?

The word "gnostic" comes from the Greek word *gnosis*, which means "knowledge" or "understanding." Gnosticism is the term long associated with a variety of similar religious movements from late antiquity that stressed secret or esoteric knowledge about the nature of the universe, human beings, and the divine. The beginnings of Gnosticism are obscure —

some believe the basic shape of the movement began shortly before the Christian era — possibly deriving from a blend of Zoroastrianism and Greek thought. Generally speaking, Gnosticism is best known as a religious competitor of orthodox Christianity in the first few centuries after Christ. Dan Brown is quite correct in saying that orthodox Christians condemned Gnostics as heretics, but he neglects to point out that the Gnostics were equally as harsh and dismissive of orthodox Christians.

One of the best scholarly books on the subject is *Gnosis: The Nature & History of Gnosticism* by Kurt Rudolph. It is required reading for most serious students of the subject, but be warned — the English translation from the original German can be pretty heavy going. In addition to his insights into the varieties of Gnostic thought, and the basic concepts they shared, Rudolph also explores the many positive contributions the Gnostics gave to early Christian thought. It is fascinating to see just how much of the New Testament was shaped by Gnostic influence and teaching. Dan Brown neglects to mention this in *The Da Vinci Code*, as if all Gnostic teaching was expunged from early Christianity by Roman imperial fiat. Quite the contrary, from a close reading of the letters of Paul and the gospel of John in the New Testament, we can see that the early church ingeniously appropriated the best ideas of Gnosticism and used them as interpretive tools to further the proclamation of the good news of Jesus.

The truth is that the New Testament is far more inclusive of differing Christian perspectives than many contemporary Christians quite realize. We are now coming to recognize that the lines between orthodoxy and heterodoxy were more blurred than we realized; there are no hard and fast rules. And, as it turns out, the New Testament is more inclusive than the canon of scriptures proposed by Marcion who, along with Fortunatus, was perhaps the most influential Gnostic teacher and theologian of the second century.

Marcion of Pontus, the son of a Christian bishop in Asia Minor, and himself then a professed Christian, argued for a narrow version of the Bible that would leave out a great many of the books that we know. He would have had only a single gospel, an abridged version of Luke, plus ten letters of Paul. There would have been no Old Testament in the Bible at all, if Marcion had had his way, because he believed that the Old Testament God was a god of vengeance and the author of all evil, while the New Testament reveals a god of grace and love. Eventually Marcion was excommunicated and set up his own rival church, claiming it as Christ's true church, but his ideas continued to circulate.

At the heart of Gnosticism lies the notion of dualism, a contrast between the evil and corrupt physical world and the cosmic world of perfect goodness. For the Gnostics, the physical world was evil: it was thought to be the flawed creation of this inferior god of the Old Testament — some even said the creator of the physical world was a fallen angel, or Satan. Gnostics called this inferior god the *demiurge*, and believed that the *demiurge* was what Christians and Jews mistakenly worshiped as God. The true God of the universe, said the Gnostics, was remote from the physical world and unknown to humankind. All that is good in the universe was believed to exist on the remote plane or sphere of this unknown God, which the Gnostics called the *pleroma*, or "fullness." Human beings were said to possess within them a divine spark from the unknown God, even though they were estranged from their proper place in the universe by the action of the *demiurge* in creating an evil world and condemning humans to it.

Although a few of the Gnostic sects embraced promiscuity, most of its followers were very austere as regards sex and marriage because of their pessimism about the created order. Women and their procreative powers were a source of evil. Enlightened knowledge of the true nature of the universe was granted only to a few elect individuals, those who because of their gift of special knowledge were able to understand things on a higher level. In other words, the Gnostics were intellectual and spiritual elitists — quite the opposite from the followers of Jesus of Nazareth.

In the same way that *The Da Vinci Code* claims that Constantine "stole Jesus," the Gnostics appropriated the Christ for their own philosophy. For them Jesus was a savior and redeemer figure who could bridge the gap between the evil world of material existence and the perfect realm of the unknown God. They ended up envisioning a very different Christ than the one whose actual followers kept the faith they had in turn received from Jesus himself. The Gnostics, in effect, *divided* Christ from the man called Jesus of Nazareth. Jesus, the Gnostics thought, was a human prophet, who had imparted secret wisdom to certain of his followers. Peter, James, John, and Thomas were often the favored elite in Gnostic writings, while others preferred Mary Magdalene, and these disciples had, in turn, passed this secret knowledge on to other followers. In their theology Christ became an entirely mythological figure, who acted out his redemptive role not on earth, but in the divine cosmic plane or sphere of the unknown God. Scholar Kurt Rudolph explains that ideas like redemption, crucifixion, and resurrection were for the Gnostics largely symbolic.[1]

It is hardly surprising that Dan Brown would be attracted to the Gnostic concept of secret knowledge being preserved and passed down from generation to generation by a hidden elect. It runs parallel to another central feature of *The Da Vinci Code*, the secret Priory of Sion that has supposedly preserved and passed down arcane knowledge about the nature of Jesus and the Holy Grail. But *The Da Vinci Code* paints a misleading picture of the Gnostics, who were not necessarily the heroic and open-minded champions of the truth, despite a tendency today to idealize them as the "free-thinkers" of their time. Nor were they underdogs suppressed and persecuted by a patriarchal apostolic church Mafia. In fact, it appears from many of the Gnostic texts themselves — which we can finally read after fifteen centuries — that they were as ready as any teachers of orthodoxy to condemn views that differed from their own.

Notable among Gnostic teachings which are offensive to thoughtful Christians is the idea that creation was the work of Satan or, at best, a fallen angel or second-class god. Gnostics typically held the Jews in contempt for their worship of Yahweh, the creator of heaven and earth. As such, it would appear from their disdain of the created order that the Gnostics were hardly "goddess worshipers." Furthermore, it is ironic that Brown cites Gnostic texts to support his claim that Jesus and Mary Magdalene enjoyed what modern people would regard as a normal married life, because Gnostics typically disdained marriage and sex for both men and women. In the

Gospel of Philip from *The Nag Hammadi Library*, we encounter a typically negative view of marriage and sex.

The Gospel of Thomas is considered the most important of the Gnostic writings that were rediscovered in the mid-twentieth century, and the pearl of the many "lost books of the Bible." What does this Gnostic work have to say about the equality of women? "Simon Peter said to them: 'Let Mary leave us, for women are not worthy of life.' Jesus said, 'I myself shall lead her in order to make her male, so that she too may become a living spirit resembling you males. For every woman who will make herself male will enter the kingdom of heaven.'"[2] Not all the Gnostic writings are so misogynistic, but it is important to remember that there are plenty of obstacles to any claim that The Gnostics were early "feminists" any more than were orthodox Christians.

Many people in the Roman Empire found this Gnostic mixture of Greek and Oriental traditions very attractive. As Christianity spread out from the Judaic world in which it was born into the Hellenistic world, it found that Gnosticism represented a serious intellectual challenge and competitor. The challenge was all the greater because there were elements in Christian teachings that could easily be mistaken for Gnostic dualism. For example, Paul frequently contrasted the "desires of the flesh" with the life-giving Spirit, as in his letter to the Romans:

> For those who live according to the flesh set their minds on the things of the flesh, but those who live according to the Spirit set their minds on the things of the Spirit. To set the mind on the flesh is death, but to set the mind on the Spirit is life and peace. (8:5-6)

How could the ascetical and disciplined elements of Christian belief be distinguished from the Gnostics' concept of human beings as cosmically estranged from God in an inherently evil world? The answer for the early church was to counter the Gnostics' claim of secret knowledge with the clear teaching of the Bible, which dated back to the beginnings of Christianity. It was in response to the Gnostic challenge, especially Marcion's "abridgement" of the canon, that the theologians and bishops of the early church sought to come to agreement about the authentic books of the Bible.

The first systematic response to Gnosticism was published in the second century by the Bishop of Lyons, Irenaeus, under the title *Against Heresies*. Irenaeus used what was becoming an authoritative number of Christian scriptures to counter the Gnostic claims of secret knowledge possessed only by an elect few. These scriptures, Irenaeus argued, were reliable because they could be traced back to the apostles. Furthermore, because they had been widely circulated throughout the empire-wide Christian movement, one could be confident that these "apostolic" scriptures were authentic and relatively unadulterated. The contrast with the scriptural tradition of the Gnostics was obvious. Unlike the early orthodox Christians, who followed the Jewish practice of protecting the exact letter of received scriptures, Gnostics were known to modify texts to suit the inspiration of whichever elect was teaching from them.

Against the Gnostic myth of an evil world created by an incompetent under-god, Irenaeus contrasted the creation story in Genesis, according to which the one and only God created heaven and earth, and human beings were created in the image of God. The world is not inherently evil, Irenaeus argued, but human beings have brought evil and death into the world through their rebellion against God. The incarnation of Christ, according to Irenaeus, was not something that happened in some distant cosmic realm but here on earth, and its purpose was to restore human beings to their proper relationship to God. Irenaeus put it this way: "By reason of his immeasurable love, Jesus Christ became what we are, in order to make us what he himself is."

Irenaeus' book did not end the conflict between orthodox Christianity and Gnosticism, for the latter persisted for centuries as part of different theological movements. In all probability, the need for Christianity to respond to the Gnostic challenge furthered the development and refinement of Christian doctrine. But, as Kurt Rudolph explains, "the gnostic schools . . . did not succeed in becoming broad mass movements — for this they were too narrow-mindedly esoteric and, above all, too hostile to the world."[3] By the sixth century Gnosticism had essentially disappeared as an organized religious movement, although Gnostic ideas continued to attract followers. For example, Manichaeanism, a form of Gnosticism that developed in Mesopotamia, persisted and even flourished in Central Asia until the Mongol invasion in the thirteenth century. The Mandaeans, a small Gnostic sect, survive today in Iraq.

The Nag Hammadi Discovery

Until recently, what we knew about the Gnostics was almost entirely based on what their opponents (such as Christian writers like Irenaeus) said about them. The Gnostics' own writings had been lost or destroyed. Then, in 1947, in the Upper Nile valley near the small town of Nag Hammadi, two farmers found a sealed jar in a jumble of boulders and rocks at the foot of a cliff. They hesitated to open it, thinking it might contain a demon, but they screwed up their courage when it occurred to them that the jar might contain gold. One of the farmers smashed the jar. What it contained were books.

The books turned out to be a library of Gnostic manuscripts. These had probably belonged to an Egyptian Gnostic community, which buried them near Nag Hammadi for safekeeping. It isn't certain when the books were buried, but a reasonable speculation is that it was in about 400 CE. By that time, the Roman Empire had become officially Christian, and it had shifted over from persecuting Christians to persecuting those whom Christians regarded as heretics.

The significance of the Nag Hammadi documents was not immediately appreciated. The farmers knew that there were rich people in Cairo who might buy them, and several of the books were sold that way. One book went to the Coptic Museum in Cairo, where it languished for years. Part of another book was bought by a Belgian antiquities dealer and eventually sold to the Jung Institute in Zurich, Switzerland. The widow of the farmer who discovered the books burned some of them in her stove, because she thought they were bad luck, or at best worthless. Eventually, the surviving books were collected, conserved, and translated. An English edition appeared in 1977, and you can read the entire translated text, along with scholarly commentaries, in *The Nag Hammadi Library* series, available in paperback.

Even though *The Da Vinci Code* calls them "scrolls," the Nag Hammadi find consists of twelve entire codices and part of a thirteenth. A codex is the familiar bound form which all modern books come in — it was usually made of papyrus. A scroll is a long roll of sheepskin. Included in the baker's dozen of codices are a total of fifty-two "tractates" in the library. Some of them, however, are versions of documents that had previously been known in other (and often better) versions. There are thirty fairly complete texts that had not been known before, plus parts of ten others. It is important to stress that at best the texts are "fairly" complete — there are gaps throughout the collection where text is missing, and some of these are extensive. For example, we have only parts of the Gospel of Mary. Where the Nag Hammadi text is the only extant version of a particular text in the collection, there is no way to fill in those gaps. In his introduction to *The Nag Hammadi Library*, James M. Robinson refers to the "physical deterioration of the books" during the fifteen hundred years that they were buried, which continued even after their discovery. He goes on to say that where the gap consists of only a few letters, it can often be filled in adequately, "but larger holes must simply remain a blank."[4]

The Nag Hammadi documents were produced in around 350 CE or later, and are written in two dialects of Coptic, which is the Egyptian language written in Greek letters. The documents are translations of earlier Greek texts, so the reliability of the Nag Hammadi documents depends in part on how good the translators were. Robinson observes that the ancient Coptic translators were not always capable of grasping the import of what they were translating. This can be seen in documents that are available in other, better translations — the Nag Hammadi documents include an excerpt from Plato's *Republic*, for example — so that scholars have some basis for comparison. Furthermore, many unintentional errors are likely to have occurred as the scribes diligently copied the texts over and over, and we have no "control copy."

None of this is intended to minimize the importance of the Nag Hammadi documents or their usefulness to scholarly investigation. But it does mean that making sense of them involves a lot more than just picking up a book off your shelf and reading a couple of selected passages, as Leigh Teabing does in *The Da Vinci Code*. Interestingly enough, in the book Teabing does not read aloud from the Nag Hammadi edition, but rather from Elaine Pagels' popular work, *The Gnostic Gospels*.

Dan Brown's novel quotes passages from two Gnostic gospels, the Gospel of Philip and the Gospel of Mary, to support his plot device that Mary Magdalene was the wife of Jesus. Before discussing these specific texts, let's clarify what these books are and what they are not.

Readers of *The Da Vinci Code* know that the authentic four gospels of Matthew, Mark, Luke, and John tell the story of the life of Jesus from four different points of view. When they read Brown's references to other "gospels," they understandably would expect that these are the same kind of document. But that is not what these "gospels" are. Neither contains — or purports to contain — any stories of Jesus' life and ministry written down very early from eyewitness accounts. Instead, the Gospel of Philip is a theological essay. What we have of the Gospel of Mary is a fragment from which scholars conclude that it originally consisted of two dialogues, one between the risen Jesus and his disciples, and the other between Mary Magdalene and the other disciples. Like the dialogues of Socrates in Plato's writings, these dialogues are probably devices to present the writer's views rather than attempts to record actual conversations.

Brown's book also claims that the Nag Hammadi and Dead Sea Scrolls are the "earliest Christian records." Where they "do not match up with the gospels in the Bible," Brown implies that this means that the biblical gospels are wrong. Of course this isn't true. First of all, the Dead Sea Scrolls are totally irrelevant to any speculation about the relationship between Jesus and Mary Magdalene. Yes, they are quite old, yet they are not "Christian records" but Jewish, and contain no Christian material of any kind. These writings are very interesting to scholars studying what is called the "intertestamental period (the time between the latest books of the Old Testament and the earliest books of the New Testament) and the religious environment into which Jesus came, but they don't talk about him at all, or about Mary Magdalene.

Second, while the Nag Hammadi documents do relate to Christianity, they were still written after the canonical gospels. Scholars are not certain whether apostles Matthew, Mark, Luke, and John actually authored the gospels attributed to them, but there is general agreement that these four gospels were written down either by them or by their associates — and certainly during the lifetimes of key eyewitnesses to the events described. The Gnostic gospels, however, including those of Philip and Mary, were written much later, long after the people whose names they bear had died. Far from being "removed" from the biblical canon, as Brown suggests, they had not even been written when the canon was largely settled. As such, with the possible exception of the Gospel of Thomas, there is no basis for considering the newly discovered Gnostic gospels to be particularly informative about the life of Jesus or his companions and disciples. Certainly there is no reason to treat them as more authoritative than the much earlier gospels of Matthew, Mark, Luke, and John.

Brown is right that the Gnostic gospels are important. It is simply that they are important in different ways than Brown claims. Let's take a closer look at the two gospels he mentions in *The Da Vinci Code*.

The Gospel of Philip

There are two men named Philip who are mentioned in the New Testament. One of the original twelve disciples was named Philip, and there was also a Philip who was selected as one of the first seven deacons appointed by the early church. It seems to have been this second Philip who became an evangelist to Samaria. The Gospel of Philip, however, was written perhaps some time after the middle of the third century, so the New Testament Philip obviously could have had no hand in writing it. The Gospel of Philip may have been given this name simply because the disciple Philip is mentioned in it, along with Matthew and Thomas.

Let's look at what the Gospel of Philip says, and compare it to the claims of *The Da Vinci Code*. Below, on the left, is *The Da Vinci Code*'s purported quotation from the Gospel of Philip ("always a good place to start," says Leigh Teabing), and on the right is the same passage from *The Nag Hammadi Library* edition. Please note that in *The Nag Hammadi Library* version, square brackets are used to show a gap in the manuscript — if the missing words can be reconstructed from the context, they appear within the brackets, but if the text cannot be reconstructed, three dots are placed within the brackets. Parentheses, ( ), are used where the translator has added material that is not in the text, but clarifies it.

As we see from the actual text, there are crucial gaps which *The Da Vinci Code* seems to have filled in all on its own.

The Da Vinci Code (p. 246)	*The Nag Hammadi Library* (p. 148)
And the companion of the Saviour is Mary Magdalene. Christ loved her more than all the disciples and used to kiss her often on her mouth. The rest of the disciples were offended by it and expressed disapproval. They said to him, "Why do you love her more than all of us?"	And the companion of the [. . .] Mary Magdalene. [. . . loved] her more than [all] the disciples [and used to] kiss her [often] on her [. . .]. The rest of [the disciples . . .]. They said to him, "Why do you love her more than all of us?" The savior answered and said to them, "Why do I not love you like her? When a blind man and one who sees are both together in darkness, they are no different from one another. When the light comes, then he who sees will see the light, and he who is blind will remain in darkness."

The holes in the text which are not so easily glossed over mean that we simply do not know whether Jesus kissed Mary on her hand, cheek, forehead, the hem of her robe, or on her mouth. And wherever he kissed her, it did not necessarily imply sexual passion. In the first century writings, people kissed for many reasons. Paul invites his friends in the Roman church to kiss one another as a sign of reconciliation and peace. The most famous kiss in the New Testament is undoubtedly the one that Judas gave Jesus in the Garden of Gethsemane when he betrayed him to the Temple guards — I doubt that even a thriller writer could make a romance out of that. Moreover, Brown leaves out Jesus' answer to the disciples' question as to why he loved Mary more than he loved them. Jesus does not ignore the question, nor does he say, "Because she is the mother of my children." He says he loves her more than the disciples because she understands his teachings better than they do — they are like blind men, while she sees the light.

Last of all, the original text uses the word "companion" to describe Mary Magdalene, not spouse. *The Da Vinci Code* claims that "any Aramaic scholar" will tell you that it "literally meant *spouse*." But the Nag Hammadi texts were not written in Aramaic — a Semitic language related to Hebrew — but in the Egyptian language of Coptic! While I don't read Coptic, I do trust esteemed Concordia professor emeritus Wesley W. Isenberg's translation of the Gospel of Philip in *The Nag Hammadi Library*, which calls Mary the "companion" of Jesus. My sense is that if the word in the Coptic text meant "spouse," Isenberg would have noted that.[5]

The Gospel of Mary

Perhaps the scholar most associated with the Gnostic Gospel of Mary is Karen King, who has written the introduction to the gospel in the *Nag Hammadi Library* edition and a well-received book on the subject. King concludes that this gospel was written some time in the second century. This makes it very old, almost as old as the biblical gospels, but Mary Magdalene could not have had a hand in writing it. King explains that only three fragmentary manuscripts are known to have survived into the modern period: two third-century fragments in Greek, and a fifth-century Coptic version, which is the one found at Nag Hammadi. The Greek manuscripts are the oldest and most trustworthy, but the Nag Hammadi manuscript, although fragmentary, is more complete.

There are important variations between the Greek and Coptic manuscripts. Notably, the Coptic variants reflect theological tendencies that arguably belong to a later time. For example, the Greek fragments seem to presume that the leadership of Mary Magdalene *as a woman* is not under debate only her teaching is challenged. The Coptic version, however, points toward a situation in which women's leadership as such is being challenged and requires defense. King's theory is that the changes in the text may reflect the historical exclusion of women from their earlier leadership roles in Christian communities.

Let's compare the passage from the Gospel of Mary that is presented in *The Da Vinci Code* with the corresponding passage in *The Nag Hammadi Library*:

Here, the passages are more similar than was the case with the Gospel of Philip, but *The Da Vinci Code* has omitted Mary's own words in response to Peter. Why would Dan Brown do that, when Mary is the centerpiece of what Teabing is telling Sophie at this point in the novel? The reason may be that

The Da Vinci Code (p. 247)	*The Nag Hammadi Library* (p. 526-7)
And Peter said, "Did the Saviour really speak with a woman without our knowledge? Are we to turn and all listen to her? Did he prefer her to us?"	Peter answered and spoke concerning these same things. He questioned them about the Savior: "Did he really speak with a woman without our knowledge (and) not openly? Are we to turn about and all listen to her? Did he prefer her to us?"
	Then Mary wept and said to Peter, "My brother Peter, what do you think? Do you think that I thought this up myself in my heart, or that I am lying about the Savior?"
And Levi answered, "Peter, you have always been hot-tempered. Now I see you contending against the woman like an adversary. If the Saviour made her worthy, who are you to reject her? Surely the Saviour knows her very well. That is why he loved her more than us.	Levi answered and said to Peter, "Peter, you have always been hot-tempered. Now I see you contending against the woman like the adversaries. But if the Savior made her worthy, who are you indeed to reject her? Surely the Savior knows her very well. That is why he loved her more than us."

Mary's words make clear that Peter was himself responding to something that Mary had just said to the disciples. If you look at the entire known text of the Gospel of Mary in the Nag Hammadi edition, you see immediately that the statement by Peter and the rejoinder by Levi are part of a larger discussion that Brown has omitted. Let's look at what precedes and what follows the short excerpt from this gospel that is quoted in *The Da Vinci Code* to better understand what the comments of Peter and Levi mean.

As Karen King points out, the Gospel of Mary in the Nag Hammadi documents is incomplete — the first six pages are missing entirely. What we have of the manuscript begins in the middle of a dialogue between the resurrected Christ and his disciples. When Christ departs, the disciples are grieved because they fear that if they "go to the gentiles and preach the gospel of the Kingdom of the Son of Man" they will be killed, as Jesus was. Mary then stands up and urges them to be resolute, because "his grace will be entirely with you and protect you." Peter says to Mary, "Sister, we know that the Savior loved you more than the rest of the women. Tell us the words of the Savior which you remember — which you know (but) we do not, nor have we heard them." Mary responds, "What is hidden from you I will proclaim to you." Mary then describes a vision that she received of Christ, telling about the ascent of a soul into the divine realms. Several pages of this discussion are missing, but we have enough to recognize it as Gnostic doctrine. Mary stops talking when she has told all that Christ spoke to her.

Then Andrew tells the disciples that he does not believe that Christ said what Mary has recounted, because "certainly these are strange ideas." Thus, the Gnostic gospel writer is using Andrew as a spokesman for the orthodox position. Peter's statement, the one quoted in *The Da Vinci Code*, follows immediately after Andrew's and is clearly intended to support the orthodox side. Mary defends herself, in the passage omitted from *The Da Vinci Code*, and Levi supports her. Levi concludes by urging the disciples to "preach the gospel, not laying down any other rule or any other law beyond what the Savior said" (presumably meaning the Gnostic doctrine). The Gospel ends (after a gap): "and they began to go forth [to] proclaim and to preach."

The Gospel of Mary is not about the personal relationship between Mary and Jesus. It is about theological differences between the orthodox and Gnostic interpretation of the Christian message, and Mary is presented as a disciple who understands the true (Gnostic) message better than Peter or Andrew.

In this chapter we have seen that the teachings of the various Gnostic schools are hardly likely to have affirmed many of *The Da Vinci Code*'s claims. From a closer inspection of the two crucial Gnostic texts cited in *The Da Vinci Code*, moreover, the facts are not in line with the book's conclusions. The novel's use of Gnostic teaching, and its references to the gospels of Philip and Mary, have little scholarly value at all. Once again, the book is downright misleading. In going beyond *The Da Vinci Code*, we learn that we have readily available resources which can tell us a great deal about the Gnostics and the Nag Hammadi library of books found in Egypt in 1947. My research has opened my eyes to the inclusiveness of the New Testament to the best ideas of Gnosticism — not the opposite. While it is true that the early church appears to have grown increasingly patriarchal in its hierarchy with every generation after Jesus' day, it still does not appear to me that the Gnostic teachers were ultimately more receptive to the ministries of women than the original gospel writers.

What can we know about women's roles in the earliest days of the church? In order to find out, we will have to consult the oldest books of the Christian movement. We will have to consult those books written between approximately 50 and 100 CE — in other words, the New Testament itself.

CHAPTER FIVE

The Sacred Feminine

The ancients believed that the male was spiritually incomplete until he had carnal knowledge of the sacred feminine. Physical union with the female remained the sole means through which man could become spiritually complete and ultimately achieve *gnosis* — knowledge of the divine....By communing with woman, man could achieve a climactic instant when his mind went totally blank and he could see God.... The Jewish Tetragrammaton YHWH — the sacred name of God — in fact derived from Jehovah, an androgynous physical union between the masculine *Jah* and the pre-Hebraic name for Eve, *Havah*. (*Da Vinci Code*, 308-9)

*T*he *Da Vinci Code* talks a great deal about the "sacred feminine." In my formal theological training, I studied a number of important contemporary feminist theologians, such as Elisabeth Schüssler Fiorenza, Phyllis Trible, Anne Carr, Sallie McFague, Deirdre Good, and Daphne Hampson. But despite my familiarity with contemporary Christian feminist thought,

I was not familiar with the term "sacred feminine" until I read *The Da Vinci Code*, although I caught on quickly to the book's interpretation of this term. *The Da Vinci Code* explains that Constantine and his successors "converted the world from matriarchal paganism to patriarchal Christianity" (*Da Vinci Code*, 124), while the Priory of Sion is described as the world's most powerful pagan goddess worship cult. Leonardo da Vinci is said to have been a leader of this secret organization devoted to these ancient worship practices. *The Da Vinci Code's* Robert Langdon explains the supposed ancient belief that the only way that a man could become "spiritually complete" was through "carnal knowledge of the sacred feminine" — or, as Sophie Neveu put it, "orgasm as prayer." The novel also includes a brief but vivid description of sexual rituals. In short, *The Da Vinci Code* appears to define the sacred feminine as neo-pagan goddess worship.

To lend a degree of historical and theological credibility to this vision of the sacred feminine, *The Da Vinci Code* argues that goddess worship is a documented part of early Jewish religion. Robert Langdon muses at one point that his Jewish students "always looked flabbergasted when he told them that the early Jewish tradition involved ritualistic sex. *"In the Temple, no less"* (*Da Vinci Code*, 309, author's emphasis). Well, I am not Jewish, but I was flabbergasted by this claim, too. No less surprising is the book's definitions of Hebrew words like Yahweh and Shekinah, the meaning of the Star of David, and Brown's claim that the ancient Israelites worshiped two gods.

Leaving Brown's claims of ritual sex in the Jewish Temple aside, let's now go beyond *The Da Vinci Code* to consider the following important theological issues. Did the ancient

Hebrews actually worship two gods, one male and one female? What *is* the biblical name of God, and what does it mean? What does that name say about the nature of the God of Abraham, Sarah, Jesus, and the two Mary's? What can we say about God from the perspective of the sacred feminine — is the One God of the Bible a male god? Or is it possible to say, from within the Bible itself, that God has long been understood in both masculine and feminine terms? In this chapter, we will take a close look at the feminine conception of God in the Bible.

Did the Hebrews Worship
Two Gods?

The Da Vinci Code argues that the ancient Hebrews actually worshiped two gods, one male and one female. For this reason the first Jewish Temple, as built by David's son Solomon, was purportedly constructed with an inner sanctum, or Holy of Holies, reserved for both the male and female deities. The book explains that "early Jews believed that the Holy of Holies in Solomon's Temple housed not only God but also His powerful female equal, Shekinah" (*Da Vinci Code*, 309). The book goes on to explain that this Holy of Holies was identified with a symbol, the Star of David, which is the intersection of two equilateral triangles — one pointed upward and the other downward. The upward triangle, called "the blade," is a masculine symbol; the downward triangle, a feminine symbol, is called "the chalice." The fusion of these two symbols, male and female, is said to signify the equality of God and his consort goddess. In *The Da Vinci Code*, the Star of David represents the union of the phallus and the chalice — the symbols for ancient Judaism's male and female gods. This notion, of course, fits perfectly with the idea of Jesus' and Mary Magdalene's alleged sexual union, and the novel is clever in weaving these various ideas together. As it explains, the best way to know God is through sacred sexual acts.

The Da Vinci Code's definition of the meaning behind the Star of David is laughable not only from the theological perspective of the Judeo-Christian tradition, but from the perspective of well-known facts as well as historical data. The idea that the ancient Hebrews believed in two gods is patently ridiculous — whether those gods are male or female — because the most basic teaching of Hebrew theology is that the God of the universe is one. Equally basic is the Hebrew notion that the One God is not to be likened to *anything* in creation — whether animal, vegetable, or mineral! Even one of *The Da Vinci Code's* most obvious contemporary sources admits that the God of Israel shared power with no female divinity, nor was that God married or betrothed to any other divinities.[1]

Yahweh

The book of Exodus, chapter three, tells a famous story about Moses and a burning bush. In that story the prophet stumbles across a bush which is continually on fire but is not consumed by the flames. A voice calls to Moses from the burning bush and engages him in one of the most important conversations in human history. It says to Moses, "I am the God of your father, the God of Abraham, the God of Isaac, and the God of Jacob." Moses is then commissioned by God to lead the Hebrew people out of bondage and slavery into freedom and the land of promise. Moses does not give in easily; he complains that no one will believe he has spoken with God. He says, "If I come to the Israelites and say to them, 'The God of your ancestors has sent me to you,' and they ask me, 'What is his name?' what shall I say to them?" God says to Moses, "I AM WHO I AM." The God of the burning bush says, "Tell them 'I AM has sent me to you . . . . YHWH, the God of your ancestors . . . has sent me to you.' This is my name forever" (Exodus 3:1-15).

From this story the Hebrews and their Christian descendants would learn the sacred name of God. It was not a proper name so much as a sentence, and one that in Hebrew is usually rendered as above, "I am who I am." But it can equally be rendered, "I will be who I will be." The divine name would be referred to in Hebrew scripture by only a four-letter acronym, YHWH, because it was thought to be blasphemous actually to write the name of God down — for fear it might be profaned. This acronym was referred to as the tetragrammaton. Although YHWH is not actually a word, over time it would become one, with vowels added to it, so that it could be pronounced by the Hebrew people. Over time it came to be pronounced something like this: "Yah-way," or Yahweh.

To me, the sacred name of God, "I will be what I will be," has a compelling internal authenticity. It tells me that the very nature of the Godhead itself is defined as "being." Twentieth-century theologian Paul Tillich called God the ultimate "Ground of Being." If God *is* the cosmic author of all that exists — time, space, matter, light, energy — then the name of

God should be nothing more and nothing less than "I am." God is. God was. God will be. God is what God is. God wills.

The root of the word "yes" is the same for "essence" and for "is." The common root of these words derive from the precursor to European languages — the so-called Proto-Indo-European tongue. Our prehistoric linguistic ancestors understood the relationship between affirmation and being, between Yes and Is. It has long been supposed that YHWH also derives from a common similar root. This may or may not be true, but to me, the essence of Godhead is the cosmic affirmation of being against a background of nothingness. God is "yes," versus a nihilist backdrop of "no." God is "yessence," as I have said to my younger students. That to me is what the sacred name means, and that is why it makes so much sense when it appears in the Old Testament.

If the sacred name of God had been revealed in the Hebrew scriptures to be anything more specific — gendered or otherwise — I might think the name were simply a human invention. As it stands, to me, there is something self-authenticating about the very lack of specificity about the name of God. I know that Jesus referred to his God as "Abba," or Daddy, but to me that was less a statement about God's gender than about his role as nurturing parent and authority. Although many patriarchal titles would accrue to the God of Israel over the centuries, such as "King" and "Lord," to me these titles reflect not the essence of the God revealed to Moses but rather the cultural assumptions of those times and places in which they were used.

Jehovah

As we saw earlier, *The Da Vinci Code* explains that "the Jewish Tetragrammaton YHWH — the sacred name of God — in fact derived from Jehovah, an androgynous physical union between the masculine Jah and the pre-Hebraic name for Eve, Havah." This statement is completely false. YHWH is not derived from Jehovah, nor is Jehovah even a Hebrew word. It is a completely artificial European construction, not biblical in any way, and at the earliest dates to the sixteenth century.

The word was invented in Europe by translators of the Bible, who for the first time were putting the sacred texts into languages other than Greek or Latin. The translators borrowed the traditional vowels associated with the Hebrew word for Lord — *adonai* — and interpolated them with the four consonants — YHWH. The result was a word sounding something like, "YaHoWa," or in Latin, "IeHoUa." There were a number of variants, partly because I's and J's and Y's were often interchangeable, and vowel sounds are written differently in European languages. But, for the most part, the first mass-produced versions of the Bible, in early modern European languages, generally put the ineffable sacred name as something like Jehovah. In 1530 William Tyndale, the English reformer and martyr, challenged the Roman Catholic decree that the Bible only exist in Latin and published a version in English. He substituted "Iehouah" for YHWH. In the 1600 Heywood Bible the word becomes "Iehove," and in the great Authorized Version of 1611, the King James Version, we find this: "That men may know that thou, whose name alone is JEHOVAH, art the Most High over all the Earth" (Psalm 83:18).

Shekinah

As we have seen, *The Da Vinci Code*'s notion that the Hebrews worshiped a powerful female God named *Shekinah*, who was the equal of the male God Yahweh, is completely false. It does raise an interesting point, however. *Shekinah* is a fascinating word, and it can be seen to have "sacred feminine" overtones that do not require us to embrace pagan goddess worship. Let us look at what the word really means, and then explore its implications for our exploration of feminine images of divinity in the Bible.

Shekinah literally means "that which dwells." Interestingly, the word is not found in the Bible at all but it represents ideas which are nonetheless rooted in Old Testament theology and tradition. We encounter the word *shekinah* in the Jewish Targums and the Talmud. The Targums are ancient translations and paraphrases of the Hebrew scriptures — almost like *Reader's Digest* versions — written in Aramaic and used in the synagogue. (Aramaic is a semitic language like Arabic, Syriac, or Hebrew — many of the words are extremely similar, as with modern day Romance languages.) They were composed to teach a basic understanding of the Bible to Jews who no longer spoke or understood biblical Hebrew. The Talmud is made up of systematic commentaries on the Mishnah, which is the law code of Judaism, and written by learned rabbis.

The word *shekinah* was used in the Targums to express — along with words for "glory" and "word" — the earthly manifestation of God's presence. For example, one Targum reads, "To the place which the Lord your God shall choose that his Shekinah may dwell there, unto the house of his Shekinah shall you seek." In the earliest strata of the Talmud — the Mishna — we encounter this example: "If two sit together and words of the Law [are spoken] between them, the Shekinah rests between them."[2]

The majority of references to *shekinah*, however, are to be found in the popular genre of rabbinical literature known as Haggadah. Haggadah is a corpus of scriptural commentary which has no formal teaching or doctrinal authority, but is used to encourage prayerfulness and piety — a form of devotional reading. In Jewish Haggadah we encounter the idea that God's visible presence in the created order — while hardly anthropomorphic or possessing any gender — may be compared to dazzling light, or "glory." This visible manifestation of divine glory would, at least in theory, be beheld by any high priest to survive an encounter with God's presence in the Holy of Holies. (No one was meant to enter this sanctum, and those who did feared death.) In the popular religious literature of the Haggadah, we see that God's nearness and presence with human beings is compared to a kind of light, a pure energy that was thought to be the manna of heaven, the food of angels. This energy was what possessed the bush that spoke to Moses, and this is what might be seen in the dwelling tabernacle of Moses or the temple of Solomon. When the temple was destroyed, the rabbinical tradition of the Pharisees would be continued without significant interruption. The Pharisees taught that God's *shekinah*, his indwelling presence, would never more be restricted to the inner sanctum of the physical temple, but exist within and between whomever loved the Law of the Lord.

The early church picked up on this notion from its Jewish origins, and we see something like *shekinah* in the New

Testament as well. God's manifestation in this world is like a celebratory and joyful light, which the Latin Church translated with the word, *"gloria."* This concept of God's dwelling presence as rejoicing light is writ large in the New Testament, especially in the letters of Paul. Paul, once a prominent Pharisee, adapted the Jewish concept of *shekinah*, God's dwelling presence and glory, as he translates it to the indwelling presence of Christ. Paul likens it to a spiritual inner light, saying, "All of us, with unveiled faces, seeing the glory of the Lord as though reflected in a mirror, are being transformed into the same image from one degree of glory to another; for this comes from the Lord, the Spirit" (2 Corinthians 3:18-19).

One of the primary teachings of Hebrew theology is that God enters into a covenant relationship with human beings by means of this indwelling presence. God's presence may be experienced by those who walk "in the light," so to speak. "Yahweh is like a lantern for my feet," says scripture. This steadfast and merciful holy presence was often compared to God building a tent in the camp of his faithful people — he would dwell steadfastly and mercifully in their presence. This notion of God's steadfastness, his unshakeable presence with his covenant people, is central to the Old Testament. Christians believe that Jesus did no more than fulfill this teaching not only for Jews, but for all human beings who allow Jesus to build a tent in their hearts.

In late Jewish Scripture, in the wisdom literature and the Apocrypha, this concept of God's *shekinah*, or dwelling presence, found further expression in terms like "the breath of God," the "wisdom of God," and the "word of God." These notions very much continued into the early Christian period, as the apostles and their followers began to make theological sense out of how God could come to dwell in the Messiah — or the "anointed one." The concept of *shekinah* clearly informs the apostolic teaching of the incarnation of Jesus through the Holy Spirit and Mary, his mother. The angel Gabriel announced to Mary that the Spirit would create within her womb the Anointed Messiah and Son of God. As Luke's gospel describes it, "The Holy Spirit will come upon you, and the power of the Most High will overshadow you" (Luke 1:35).

Stoic and Platonic thought greatly influenced first-century Jewish and Christian thinkers. It taught that the universe was created by the Logos, or the "Word" of God. Jewish thinkers began to merge their biblical notions of Holy Wisdom, *shekinah*, and the luminescent breath of God's creating word with the philosophical concept of the Logos. By the time of Jesus' birth, this understanding was well established, and it informed the early Christian writers who borrowed from the predominant Greek philosophical vocabulary as they explored the mystery of Jesus. As we see in the Gospel of John, this philosophical terminology is used in the very first chapter: "In the beginning was the Word, and the Word was with God and the Word was God. He was in the beginning with God. All things came into being through him . . . . And the Word became flesh and lived among us, and we have seen his glory" (John 1:1-3, 14).

Can We Find the Sacred Feminine in the Bible?

The Da Vinci Code ingeniously appropriates a number of terms and ideas from biblical theology to bolster the argument that respecting the sacred feminine means embracing pagan goddess worship. Brown borrows a number of valid ideas from biblical thought — such as the name of YHWH and the concept of *shekinah* — but he defines them incorrectly. To me, this distortion of these sacred words — one clearly gender-neutral, the other more feminine — has plainly led many of his readers to wonder and even to question their faith.

However, I know that many readers have been attracted to *The Da Vinci Code* because they feel that it offers a feminist alternative to patriarchal mainstream religion. These readers have a legitimate concern. It is unfortunately true that Christianity, like Judaism and Islam, has had a strong tendency toward patriarchy for much of its history. I think this has begun to change in Christianity and Judaism (Islam is beyond the scope of this discussion) and I am grateful for that, but the transformation is by no means complete. Yet, as prominent feminist Christian scholars attest, you don't have to jettison Christianity and Judaism, or the Bible, in order to find the sacred feminine. There is plenty of "feminine" material in our scriptures, including material about feminine attributes of the God of Abraham, Sarah, Jesus, and the Mary's. Rather than abandon our religious traditions in favor of pagan goddess worship, as Brown's book would have us do, we should go beyond *The Da Vinci Code* to rediscover the sacred feminine in Christian and Jewish scriptures.

Take the concept that we were just examining, *shekinah*. Although *shekinah* is not the name of a female deity, as *The Da Vinci Code* claims, the word does embrace feminine aspects of the one God. The concept of God's wisdom in late Jewish and early Christian scripture has always been regarded as a feminine idea: the female name Sophia actually comes from the Greek word for wisdom. Similarly, Gloria is both a female name and a Latin word meaning the shining light of God's presence — quite akin to *shekinah*, in fact.

It is true that in western Christianity, the Holy Spirit is traditionally regarded as masculine. But following my own brand of Celtic-inspired Anglican Christianity, there is something clearly feminine about the Sacred Spirit (or Breath) of God. To my way of thinking, there is also a maternal dimension to the ever-abiding, ever-caring, ever-nurturing presence of God. This is what I teach to my parishioners, my friends, and my youngsters. This is what I will teach my daughter. That is not merely because I personally wish it were part of our Christian tradition — but because it always has been. I teach a feminine perspective of God because it is in the very Hebrew and Christian scriptures I call sacred.

Consider the following verses from both the Hebrew and Christian scriptures:

- **Isaiah 66:12-13:** "For thus says the LORD: I will extend prosperity to her like a river, and the wealth of the nations like an overflowing stream; and you shall nurse and be carried on her arm, and dandled on her knees. As a mother comforts her child, so I will comfort you; you shall be comforted in Jerusalem."

- **2 Esdras 1:28-30:** "Thus says the Lord Almighty: Have I not entreated you as a father entreats his sons or a mother her daughters or a nurse her children, so that you should be my people and I should be your God, and that you should be my children and I should be your father? I gathered you as a hen gathers her chicks under her wings."

- **Wisdom of Solomon 7:22-25:** "There is in [Wisdom] a spirit that is intelligent, holy, unique, manifold, subtle, mobile, clear, unpolluted, distinct, invulnerable, loving the good, keen, irresistible, beneficent, humane, steadfast, sure, free from anxiety, all-powerful, overseeing all, and penetrating through all spirits that are intelligent, pure, and altogether subtle. For wisdom is more mobile than any motion; because of her pureness she pervades and penetrates all things. For she is a breath of the power of God, and a pure emanation of the glory of the Almighty."

- **Sirach 15:1-3:** "Whoever holds to the law will obtain wisdom. She will come to meet him like a mother, and like a young bride she will welcome him. She will feed him with the bread of learning, and give him the water of wisdom to drink."

- **Matthew 23:37; Luke 13:34:** [Jesus said,] "Jerusalem, Jerusalem, the city that kills the prophets and stones those who are sent to it! How often have I desired to gather your children together as a hen gathers her brood under her wings, and you were not willing!"

Modern day feminist theologians are not the first to emphasize these dimensions of scripture, either. One of Anglican Christianity's most beloved spiritual writers is Julian of Norwich. She lived in England about a century before Leonardo da Vinci's time, and published a manuscript of mystical writings at the end of the fourteenth century. Her book, *Showings of Divine Love,* is based on her mystical revelation from God in May of 1373. At the heart of her writings is a theology about the dual nature of human existence — we are "substantial" beings united in relationship with the Creator, but we are also sensual beings limited to varying degrees by our life in this world, where we do not always perceive or accept God's love. According to Julian, "substance" and "sensuality" are made one in Christ by the events of his incarnation, passion and death, and resurrection. Julian makes very striking use of a fairly common medieval image of Christ as mother. Here is what she says in her *Showings:*

> I saw that God rejoices to be our Father, and also that he rejoices to be our Mother . . . . We make our humble complaint to our beloved Mother, and he sprinkles us with his precious blood, and makes our soul pliable and tender, and restores us to our full beauty in the course of time . . . . Beautiful and sweet is our heavenly Mother.

CHAPTER SIX

Powerful Christian
Women

The Grail is literally the ancient symbol for woman-
hood, and the *Holy* Grail represents the sacred feminine and the goddess, which of course has now been
lost, virtually eliminated by the Church. The power of
the female and her ability to produce life was once
very sacred, but it posed a threat to the rise of the pre-
dominantly male Church, and so the sacred feminine
was demonized and called unclean. (*Da Vinci Code*,
238)

*T*he Da Vinci Code presents a stark dichotomy between its
essentially pagan vision of the sacred feminine and what
it calls a "defeminized" Christianity. The church, we are told,
has "virtually eliminated" the sacred feminine. Indeed, this
apparently pro-feminist stance is perhaps why so many contemporary readers have been interested in the book. Certainly
all churches can still be quite sexist and narrow-minded these
days, and the Roman Catholic Church is by no means the only

denomination with that attitude. And yet I have found *The Da Vinci Code* to be an insult to feminist theology and scholarship.

The novel claims that the church has long suppressed the real truth about the roles of women and notions of the sacred feminine, which is a true statement. But then, instead of using real historical data to back up the claim, the *The Da Vinci Code* either invents or ignores the facts. For example, Brown claims that in its effort to stamp out any vestige of the sacred feminine, the church has murdered five million women — "all female scholars, priestesses, gypsies, mystics, nature lovers, herb gatherers, and any women 'suspiciously attuned to the natural world.'"[1] The book then presents us with an absurd view of Mary Magdalene, primarily lifted from pulp non-fiction like *Holy Blood, Holy Grail*, and a few misinterpreted snippets of Gnostic literature. At the same time, *The Da Vinci Code* completely ignores the long-established role of Mary the Mother of Jesus in Christian teaching, practice, and piety, as well as significant Christian women disciples mentioned by name in the New Testament itself.

Anyone with access to a copy of the New Testament and who knows where to look can find the names and roles of influential women in the earliest era of the church. No one needs to consult non-biblical texts, Gnostic or otherwise, to come up with an encouraging picture of women's ministries in the early church. The New Testament itself paints a more historical picture of women's early ministries than any other source from the first century. The sad news, which must be acknowledged by the church, is that these names and the importance of women's ministries at all levels have been suppressed by many Christian leaders through the ages led by their own sexist assumptions and biases. The past fifty years of feminist scholarship have done a good deal to lift women's ministries out of obscurity, but these scholars have not had to *invent* something that was not there from the beginning — just as the New Testament reveals.

As we saw in the previous chapter, Christian and Jewish scriptures give plenty of recognition to the feminine aspects of God. In this chapter as we go beyond *The Da Vinci Code*, we will explore the truth about the women who were active in the early church.

Women in the Early Church

The evidence for women's roles in the earliest church is somewhat mixed. But there is still plenty of material in the New Testament itself about women doing all sorts of powerful ministry in the early days. Notably, in the oldest texts of the New Testament, we find a treasure trove of material. In Paul's letters letter to the church in Galatia, a Roman province in Asia Minor, he writes, "In Christ there is neither male nor female." We also find Paul's mention of many women by name, and a brief description of their ministries, particularly in his greetings to local congregations toward the end of his letter to the Romans (16:1ff):

- "I commend to you our sister Phoebe, a deacon of the church, . . . so that you may welcome her in the Lord as is fitting for the saints, and help her in whatever she may require from you, for she has been a benefactor of many and of myself as well."

- "Greet Prisca and Aquila, who work with me in Christ Jesus, and who risked their necks for my life, to whom not only I give thanks, but also all the churches of the Gentiles. Greet also the church in their house . . ."
- "Greet Mary, who has worked very hard among you."
- "Greet Andronicus and Junia, my relatives who were in prison with me; they are prominent among the apostles, and they were in Christ before I was . . ."
- "Greet one another with a holy kiss . . .I urge you brothers and sisters, to keep an eye on those who cause dissensions and offenses . . ."

This is very revealing. Paul is writing not to some small, marginalized church at the edges of the empire, but to the Church at Rome — the Church at Rome which would become, one day, the dominant branch of Christianity, and whose episcopacy would become the papacy. How amazing that in this letter, dating to the 50s, a woman Junia is called "an apostle" in the early Roman Church.

For many years, church scholars debated whether or not this could possibly be a woman's name — many argued that the name should have been "Junias," which is a masculine variant. But, despite those claims, the best ancient manuscripts have the name as Junia, a female name. Paul says Junia was "in Christ before I was," which means that she became a Christian before he did. This is fascinating, too. Since Paul was converted within a few years of the resurrection, a likely conclusion would have to be that Junia was one of the very earliest converts to Christianity. Insofar as she is identified as part of the Roman church, and that church was founded before Paul and Peter arrived there, she must have been one of the founding members of the church at Rome. If Paul is referring to her as an "apostle," it is very possible that she had been in Jerusalem at the time of Jesus' passion and resurrection. Following the account of Pentecost in Acts, maybe Junia was one of the "visitors from Rome" who heard the gospel from those Spirit-filled witnesses.

So what did early women leaders like those mentioned in Romans do in the church? Well, the earliest Christian communities met in people's houses; they did not have churches for quite some time. The New Testament tells us that some women owned the houses in which early Christians often met, so presumably these were women of some wealth and position. As patrons of the nascent community, they would have had influence.

The Book of Acts also reminds us of the ministry of Tabitha. During Peter's travels to young churches in Lydda and Joppa, which are recorded in the Book of Acts, he encountered "a disciple whose name was Tabitha, which in Greek is Dorcas. She was devoted to good works and acts of charity." When Dorcas suddenly became ill and died, the disciples sent for Peter in nearby Lydda, and when he arrived in Joppa they took him to the room where Dorcas lay, ready for burial. "All the widows stood beside him, weeping and showing tunics and other clothing that Dorcas had made while she was with them. Peter put all of them outside, and then he knelt down and prayed. He turned to the body and said, 'Tabitha, get up.' Then she opened her eyes, and seeing Peter, she sat up. He gave her his hand and helped her up. Then calling the saints and widows, he showed her to be alive. This became known throughout Joppa, and many believed in the Lord" (Acts 9:36-42).

This passage from Acts is fascinating. First of all, Tabitha is called a disciple — the only time the term applies to a woman in Acts. Second, she is running a ministry for widows and those in need. In that patriarchal society, widows and unmarried women had little social or economic value, and these unprotected women often fell through the cracks with no support at all. It appears that Tabitha made clothes for these women, and other needy souls. As such, her death was a crisis for them. Nobody else would help them. It appears that the message of this story is that the early church heard their cries, and sent Peter, the leader, to respond. His healing of the disciple Tabitha was a prophetic reassurance that the power of Christ is for the poor, the forgotten, the widowed, and the marginalized. Whatever Peter's views on the ministry of women, he certainly respected the value, dignity, and authority of the woman he raised from the dead.

Let us now delve deeper and examine perhaps the two most important women in the early church.

Mary Magdalene

Despite *The Da Vinci Code*'s many claims to the contrary, there is no solid historical evidence from which we can construct a detailed picture of Mary Magdalene's life. Moreover, there is no basis in fact, history, or scripture to claim that Mary Magdalene and Jesus ever married, conceived children, kissed, or even held hands. *The Da Vinci Code* uses non-biblical texts like the Gospel of Mary to claim that Mary Magdalene was exalted over the male disciples of Jesus, and the Gospel of

Philip to claim she was Jesus' lover. But, as we saw in the previous chapter, these texts are of dubious factual value when it
comes to learning about the historical Mary Magdalene.

That leaves us with the New Testament gospels, and unfortunately, they don't say very much about this powerful figure.
They do tell us her name, however, and where she was from.
Mary's biblical name was Miriam, and she came from the small
fishing town of Magdala on the Sea of Galilee where Jesus
went preaching and healing. It appears that Mary of Magdala
was part of Jesus' inner circle of followers. She is mentioned as
such in Luke's gospel, being one who accompanied Jesus in his
travels as an itinerant preacher and healer. The relevant passage says, "The Twelve were with him, as well as some women
who had been cured of evil spirits and infirmities: Mary, called
Magdalene, from whom seven demons had gone out" (Luke
8:1-2). Luke does not announce this with great fanfare, but
how remarkable that Jesus had women among his followers in
that patriarchal time and society.

The earliest gospel of them all, Mark, does not mention
anything about Mary of Magdala until the last week of Jesus'
life. The same is true of the Gospel of Matthew. In the Gospel
of John, which inspired Leonardo's painting of the Last Supper,
the Magdalene does not appear until the crucifixion itself. So,
Luke is really the only source of data about her from before the
passion of Jesus. And that is enough, surely, to say that she was
one of Jesus' followers and companions in his ministry.

From Luke's sole account of her beginnings with Jesus'
band of followers, it would appear that Mary may have been
involved in spiritual activity of a darker sort before meeting
Jesus. The passage from Luke tells us that Jesus cast seven

demons out of Mary of Magdala, a possible clue that she had been involved in sorcery or other esoteric arts. That said, there is absolutely no reason to believe that the Magdalene disciple was a prostitute, a legend circulating from the time of Pope Gregory the Great, who erroneously declared that Mary of Magdala was the anonymous prostitute who anointed Jesus' feet in Luke 7. The Catholic Church has taught for over a thousand years that Mary of Magdala was a fallen woman, but has taken this back in recent years, seeking to correct the mistake. That correction may rightly be judged "too little, too late," for many of us, and for those of us who wish to know more about her, sadly, we probably never will.

After Luke's account of her travels with the disciples, there is no mention of Mary of Magdala again until the last week of Jesus' life. There simply is no way to know what happened in the interim — unless a lost scripture is discovered which is far more authentic and ancient than anything in the Nag Hammadi library. The story of Mary of Magdala picks up again with her traveling with Jesus and the Twelve from Galilee to Jerusalem to prepare for the Passover. And really, it is in the events of that final week of Jesus' life that Mary becomes the apostolic figure she was in the nascent church, being Jesus' witness and faithful servant at the crucifixion, resurrection, and beyond.

In Mark we encounter Mary of Magdala as one of the group of women who traveled to Jerusalem with Jesus, and provided for his needs. She witnessed the crucifixion as well, after the male disciples had all denied, betrayed, or deserted Jesus. Later in the Gospel of Mark, Mary of Magdala and Mary the Mother of God went to where Jesus was buried, in the tomb of

Joseph of Arimathea. There, while trying to anoint his body, they witnessed the empty tomb and the presence of an angel. Roughly the same story appears in Matthew and John. Many have thought that the Gospel of John's account of the resurrection serves to "authenticate" the gospel narratives of Jesus' resurrection — who would make up a story that has Jesus appearing first of all to a woman from whom he had cast out seven demons? This account of Mary of Magdala's witness to the resurrection is just as inspiring now as it was in the very beginning, when she told the other disciples what she had witnessed.

Mary of Magdala was commissioned by Jesus to tell the others what was going on, and in that she became the "apostle to the apostles," bearing the witness and news of a risen Lord. In the Gospel of John, she is really the first apostle of the Good News, because she is the first to tell anyone of it. We know nothing more about her in the New Testament, but it appears obvious that she was revered by the evangelists of the early church in whose books she becomes the first bearer of Good News. While we wish we could know more about her biography, as with Jesus and others, the New Testament only gives us what the early church thought we needed to know.

Mary the Mother of Jesus

Though it is true that Mary Magdalene has not been given her full due as an early apostle in most quarters, for two millennia the majority of Christians around the globe have highly exalted Mary the mother of Jesus. The figure of Mary is central to

Roman and Orthodox piety, and she is extremely important for many Anglicans as well. Even Protestant Evangelicals will recognize the unique role of Mary as the mother of the Incarnate Word — despite Reformation-style reservations about "popish" devotion to saints and relics. According to the minimum standard of the faith shared by *all* Christians — the New Testament — Jesus' mother is unavoidably significant. She is the heart of the New Testament's witness to the sacred feminine as the first Christian and model of Christ-like faithfulness. She is *the* archetype of the "Christian feminine divine," whether one takes that metaphorically or literally.

Christians disagree about the biographical details of the Virgin Mary. The New Testament gives us frustratingly little data about her. We know who she was and that she actually lived. To fill the gap, and to feed their hunger for more information, many Roman Catholics uphold a number of non-biblical texts about the Virgin Mary. While these are not *Gnostic* texts, they are ancient texts of questionable authenticity or apostolic origin, such as the *Protoevangelion of James*, the *Transitus Mariae*, and others. Protestants do not turn to these texts for doctrine, restricting themselves only to the New Testament canon of twenty-seven books. Orthodox Christians value a number of extra-biblical traditions, as well, as do the Christians of Ethiopia — who arguably have the most books in their canon of scripture (thirty-five in all) of any Christian group. It is noteworthy that Roman Catholics teach that Mary was a perpetual virgin, while most Protestants believe she led a normal sexual life with her husband after the birth of Jesus.

Regardless of the exact particulars of her life, her ultimate and universal Christian importance stems from her faithfulness to the will of God, her nurture and support of the incarnate Word, her sacrifice of excruciating sorrow upon the death of her first-born son on Calvary, and her witness to the resurrection. Moreover, the faithful and skeptics alike have every scholarly reason to accept as factual that she was the "mother" of the entire first generation of Christian apostles and disciples.

All told, whether one is Catholic, Orthodox, Protestant, or Anglican, it is impossible to overlook the "sacred femininity" of the Virgin Mary. But in making its case for the sacred feminine, *The Da Vinci Code* ignores her completely. Let us go again beyond *The Da Vinci Code*, and look closer at Mary the mother of God.

Christian Devotion to Holy Mary

Christian devotion to the Virgin Mary is documented as early as the first century, in the New Testament itself. In the gospels' account of God's plan for human salvation, Mary plays a central role. The "nativity stories" of Matthew and Luke portray her as the mother of the Savior. In Luke's gospel, the mother of John the Baptist, Elizabeth, refers to Mary as nothing less than the queen-mother of a Messiah-king — high praise coming in the very first century of the Christian era. A decade or two later, the Christian community associated with the apostle John — the Beloved Disciple and adoptive son of Mary after Jesus' death and resurrection — already looked upon Mary as the archetypal figure for faithful Christian behavior.

In the second century clerical authority became the domain of men only, but the spiritual power of Mary, a kind of "feminine divine," grew and spread. It appears that while the developing Christian hierarchy could not overcome the patriarchal norms of society, feminine aspects of divinity also held their own through special devotion to Mary. In early Roman Christian art, creeds, and prayers, Mary "the mother of God," grew in importance.

The great second-century bishop Irenaeus of Lyon compared Mary to a second Eve, and Jesus to a second Adam. Irenaeus is significant as a third-generation Christian: in his boyhood, Irenaeus knew Polycarp, a saint burned to death in old age for his faith in Christ. Polycarp was thought to have studied under John the Beloved Disciple, who took care of the Virgin Mary until her death. Irenaeus, who did much to build Christianity in early France, dedicated his life to refuting heterodox Gnostic teaching. Among his greatest theological contributions to Christian thought was to remind everybody, against the teaching of Marcion, that the God of the Old and New Testaments was the same God — that the God of the Jews, of Abraham, Sarah and Isaac, was the God of Joseph, Mary and Jesus. That same God took human form by the assent of Mary, and became one of us, in fulfillment of the Hebrew scriptures. Irenaeus' emphasis on the incarnation of God's word in Christ came in response to Gnostic teaching that Christ was not truly human, but merely a human apparition. By focusing on the human reality of Jesus, Irenaeus teaches that as the mother of the fully human and fully divine Jesus, Mary must therefore be called the "God-bearer." Thanks to Irenaeus, the sacred feminine is upheld, not denied. Moreover, Mary's place at the center of God's plan of redemption is defended.

Two centuries later, after the reign of Constantine, the place of Mary in Christian thought continued to flourish. Despite the far-fetched claims of *The Da Vinci Code* that Constantine invented the divinity of Christ and downplayed any appreciation of the sacred feminine, Mary's star continued to rise in church doctrine and practice in the fourth and fifth centuries. Athanasius, the theologian who defended so much of the doctrine overwhelmingly upheld at the Council of Nicaea, proposed the Virgin Mary as the prime role model for all female divines, or nuns. Among many such "holy virgins," as nuns were then called, were powerful women who estab-lished prominent ministries throughout the Christianized Roman world. One such figure was Olympias, who in the late fourth century ran a number of convents, clinics, and other ministries in Constantinople. She was John Chrysostom's advi-sor, and to some extent his greatest assistant in ministry — for she was extraordinarily rich. Another contemporary of hers was St. Ambrose, archbishop of Milan, who wrote a gorgeous work comparing Mary to Helena, the mother of Constantine. Rather than diminishing either woman's stature, he elevated them to new heights. In Ambrose's funeral oration for Emperor Theodosius in 395, he linked the two feminine divines in the Christian imagination. Ultimately, at the Council of Ephesus in 431, a statement was made, which most Christians still uphold — Mary was honored with the title of "*theotokos,*" or "God-bearer." Without her consent to the Holy Spirit, the incarnation of God in Jesus would never have taken place.

Throughout the ancient church, Christian devotion to Mary stemmed primarily from the notion that she was the God-bearer. But in the early Middle Ages, Mary was transformed from exalted bearer of God into an omnipotent divine figure in her own right. She became not merely a devotional figure but rather a semi-divine figure who answered prayers and interceded actively on behalf of those who turned to her. In other words, she became a portal into the divine and, for many Christians, nothing less than another face of God Almighty. It can be argued that through the Middle Ages Mary became a part of the Godhead in the minds of many Christians. So, quite the opposite of what *The Da Vinci Code* argues, Mary's role as "sacred feminine" grew to new heights not present in the earliest strata of the church. The Second Council of Nicaea, which was held in 787, made the following statement and it is still valid for all Orthodox Christians:

> The Lord, the apostles and the prophets have taught us that we must venerate in the first place the Holy Mother of God, who is above all the heavenly powers . . . . If any one does not confess that the holy, ever virgin Mary, really and truly the Mother of God, is higher than all creatures visible and invisible, and does not implore, with a sincere faith, her intercession, given her powerful access to our God born of her, let him be anathema.

By the fifteenth century, a dozen centuries after Constantine's supposedly "patriarchal usurpation of the human Jesus," it would appear that many pious Catholics *acted* as if they believed in a God with four dimensions — Father, Mother, Holy Spirit, and Jesus. In Leonardo's century, the invention of the printing press increased the diffusion of Marian devotional materials and artwork. Leonardo's drawing of Mary and her mother Anne is highly devotional, focusing as it does on the women rather than on the infant Jesus or the infant Baptist. In the seventeenth and eighteenth centuries, even after the Enlightenment began, devotion to Mary flowered and expanded in Europe. Many believers fixed Mary at the center of their devotional life and piety. In France, a school of Marian-inspired spirituality flourished under the guidance of a Roman Catholic prince of the church, Cardinal de Bérulle. Bérulle followed the inspiration of his saintly spiritual cousin, Barbe Jeanne Acarie, who took the name "Mary of the Incarnation" when she became a Carmelite nun. They taught that Mary is intimately intertwined in the mystery of the Word made flesh — and is just as central to saving belief as Jesus. That school of spirituality would be headed later on by the parish priest of the Church of Saint-Sulpice, Jean-Jaques Olier, in whose church an exciting scene from *The Da Vinci Code* takes place. Mary's redemptive role was also underscored in the eighteenth century by St. Alphonse de Ligouri, whose writings emphasize that even as Mary offered up her son's life on the cross for our sakes, so does she "collaborate" in the salvation of humankind.

The Passion of Mary and Jesus

Let us turn our attention to a very interesting work of art, from late seventeenth-century Italy, which reflects these ideas not in books or documents, but in oil on copper for all to see. *The Passion of Mary and Jesus* is a striking painting, and it is a perfect example of extreme devotion to Mary. Unlike Leonardo's

Last Supper, which depicts a commonly treated scene from the Bible, the subject of *this* painting is rather unique: it portrays Mary following Jesus on the road to Calvary, shouldering her own cross.

I have shown the image to a number of scholars, and none has seen anything quite like it. Unfortunately little is known about this anonymous work. Scholars date the painting to the second half of the seventeenth century, and think that it comes from northern Italy. It has been identified as belonging to the Lombard School, and it may have come from a studio near Milan. It is a small piece, (11.5" x 14.25"), painted with oil on copper.

When I first saw *The Passion of Mary and Jesus* in a private collection I was astounded. Its owner was puzzled by it, too, and called me over for a theologically trained opinion of its meaning and Christian context. He asked me, "Is this a scene from the Bible?" Seeing Mary carrying her own cross right behind Jesus, I had to say, "Well, it is not a scene from the Bible, but it does teach a biblical notion."

How so?

In this painting of Mary and Jesus, each is carrying a cross of the same size and Mary is following behind Jesus. They are wearing almost identical clothing — except for her head covering, which fits standard iconographic conventions. They are each bare-footed; they are each the same height; their posture is identical. They take up the same amount of space on the image, and their faces both wear the same expression of patient suffering. In fact the two figures appear to be nearly identical, each sharing equal prominence within the context of the image itself. This is rather astounding considering that it is nowhere stated in the Bible that Jesus and Mary were equals or that she carried her own cross.

Certainly, this painting is not a visual depiction of a biblical event like Leonardo's *Last Supper*. To those who object to Marian devotion, *The Passion of Mary and Jesus* appears to depict the controversial teaching that Mary's role in the salvation of the world is no less *necessary* than Jesus' role. That argument holds that she agreed to bear Jesus Christ into the world, and it was her little boy who was tortured and murdered before her very eyes. As such, Mary's emotional pain on Calvary was its own kind of crucifixion, its own ultimate sacrifice. As John Chrysostom wrote in the fourth century, "Whoever then was present on the Mount of Calvary might see two altars, on which two great sacrifices were consummated; the one in the body of Jesus, the other in the heart of Mary." But the painting also seems to depict metaphorically a simple New Testament teaching. As Jesus said, "If you will be my disciple, die to yourself, take up your cross, and follow me."

We see that in the New Testament there is compelling evidence for the roles of women in all levels of Christian ministry in the earliest years of the church. These women were not merely spouses of apostles and disciples, but apostles and disciples themselves. The Bible we read today, the vast majority of whose books were collected by the end of the first century, confirms this beyond a shadow of a doubt. There may yet be lost scriptures which will give us an even richer understanding of the roles of women in the Christian community — but the ones that have been discovered so far tell us very little of those early days. They indicate how and why women lost authority in the church hierarchy, but nothing new about the roles they originally had. Despite all the excitement of the discovery and study of the lost Gnostic gospels, they don't tell us anything substantive about Mary Magdalene or Jesus as historical figures. Moreover, the vast majority of Catholics and Orthodox Christians have revered the sacred feminine aspects of God and the early saints in devotion to Mary Magdalene, Mary the Mother of Jesus, and many other female divines through the centuries. Devotional art illustrates this, and in at least one rather unique example, *The Passion of Mary and Jesus*, it shows the extent to which women were revered by Christians.

CHAPTER SEVEN

Did Jesus Marry
Mary Magdalene?

Behold...the greatest cover-up in human history. Not only was Jesus Christ married, but He was a father. My dear, Mary Magdalene was the Holy Vessel. She was the chalice that bore the royal bloodline of Jesus Christ. She was the womb that bore the lineage, and the vine from which the sacred fruit sprang forth! (*Da Vinci Code*, 249).

I am a Christian, and I am a priest. As someone who has been taught by other Christians from Honduras to Rwanda, from South Dakota to North Carolina, I have seen that Christ comes in a multitude of shapes, sizes, races, and sexes, and like to think I am truly open to wisdom from wherever it comes. I believe much can be learned about God and even more about humanity from religious traditions other than my own— including those early variations of apostolic Christianity that did not survive antiquity. I also like to think I am orthodox because I believe, obey, and carry on the apostolic formulations of the core doctrines of my faith. I believe in the humanity and divinity of Christ. I believe that the New Testament and the Hebrew Scriptures are the most blessed books of the Judeo-Christian religious heritage and that they contain all things necessary to an eternally life-giving relationship with the One God. I believe that the mind of Christ is revealed in the whole of the Bible, and is not as well witnessed to by any other ancient texts — Gnostic, Christian, or otherwise. Other texts and traditions may range from good to great, but they are neither necessary nor superior in value. As this kind of Christian, I have two responses to *The Da Vinci Code*, one contentious and one collaborative.

First, as I have shown, I am troubled by the book's attempts to rewrite history and reshape the heart of Christianity. While it is a noble cause to recover lost truths and wrongfully suppressed ideas, this book does an ignoble job of it — plumbing historical and spiritual mysteries for obviously commercial ends. Instead of honestly pointing out Christianity's numerous historical sins, *The Da Vinci Code* largely fabricates its case against the church.

Principal among the book's dubious indictments is this claim that nearly everything the church has taught about Christ is false. We are told that a systematic effort to divinize Jesus and to marginalize the sacred feminine has obscured the historical fact that Jesus of Nazareth and Mary Magdalene were actually a married couple who produced children. This claim is positioned as not only factual, but also somehow more enlightened than traditional Christian teachings about them. The book scoffs at the traditional notion that Jesus was not married to anyone.

Apparently, it is not good enough for Christians to teach that Mary Magdalene was one of Jesus' most important witnesses, companions, and spiritual friends. *The Da Vinci Code* teaches on the contrary that for the sacred feminine to be honored by Christians, we must deny the divinity of Jesus and accept his marriage and procreation of children with Mary Magdalene. This claim of historical and spiritual "gnosis" forms the central thread of the entire book. But, as we have shown, *The Da Vinci Code*'s case for the marriage of Jesus and Mary Magdalene is poor. And aside from the weakness of the book's argument, there is no good argument outside *The Da Vinci Code*, either. Indeed, there is much more evidence against this claim than for it, whether one believes in God or not.

Ironically, there is nothing about the idea of a married Jesus that would undermine the basic Christian faith. Even if it *could* be proven that Jesus and Mary Magdalene were married, it would hardly undo the key Christian claims as found in such formulations as the Nicene Creed because the apostolic faith — by whatever name it is called, whether catholic, biblical, or orthodox — holds that Jesus was fully human and fully divine. Given that first-century Jewish rabbis were typically married, and Jesus was regarded as a wise man and a teacher, it would have been perfectly normal for Jesus to have taken a wife. There was no cultural expectation that holy men *needed* to be single. We also know Jesus' teachings on marriage and that his first miracle took place at a wedding in Cana, where he turned water into wine. But since we believe that Jesus' full humanity does not diminish his full divinity, it becomes moot whether or not he was married or single. Just as today, at least in my church, we do not believe married people are any more fully human than single people are.

What does bother me is the notion that for Mary Magdalene to be fully significant, she had to be married. Compared to Dan Brown's argument about a married Mary Magdalene, the New Testament seems far more enlightened. For it is totally obvious that the New Testament's very high view of Mary Magdalene's status as a disciple rests entirely on her faithfulness alone, quite apart from questions of her marital status.

From the Code to the Truth

Now, my second response to *The Da Vinci Code* is quite positive. There is just something about the book that fascinates people. As such, the book is a publishing and cultural phenomenon that creates a unique teaching opportunity by setting free a remarkable torrent of popular interest in historical, biblical, and theological issues previously ignored by the wider public. Until *The Da Vinci Code*, the only people talking about the formation of the Bible, lost scriptures, Gnosticism, and Mary Magdalene were academics, clergy, and a minority of folks on society's intellectual fringe. Certainly there were pop books like *Holy Blood, Holy Grail* or *Templar Revelation* that sold well, but intelligent and scholarly books by reputable scholars on similar themes did not take the culture by storm. There are plenty of controversial but still sound books exploring lost scriptures, variant forms of Christianity and early heresies, and feminist approaches to the Bible, and they are worth reading. To name a few, Robert Eisenman's study, *James the Brother of Jesus*, is an exhaustive examination of alternative Christianities within the apostolic period. Of similar value is Elaine Pagels' classic, *The Gnostic Gospels*, and Bart Ehrman's *Lost Christianities*. Yet as good as these books are for their style and scholarship, you probably won't see people reading them by the swimming pool or on an airplane. Instead, you will see *The Da Vinci Code*.

In seeking to go beyond *The Da Vinci Code* in order to teach people whom it has both touched and fascinated, I have had to ask myself, "Why is this book so interesting to people?" I think there are four reasons. First of all, people are naturally intrigued by secrets and conspiracies. We believe today that there are a many great secrets that have been kept from us by those in positions of power. This idea is so widespread, that in today's culture it is no longer considered *radical* to question authority. Indeed, I would say it is a normative assumption in our culture. A generation after the 1960s counter-cultural revolution, it is mainstream practice to want to overturn whatever authoritarian structures remain, and uncover whatever secrets are hidden beneath. In this country, at least, everything from popular music to academic discovery is typically packaged as "revolutionary" or "all new." Only in today's society does *alternative* music become mainstream. The same is true in the academy, where so many scholars seem to operate with a "counter-cultural" or "deconstructionist" approach. It is as if we are all debunkers in today's world — even me, as I write this book. From right-wing conspiracy nuts in Idaho to left-wing theoreticians in France, it seems that everybody is hungry to get the real, hidden, lost, "gnosis." And certainly, *The Da Vinci*

Code offers a powerful set of ideas for those who want to learn the "real truth."

In the second place, many readers today are suspicious of the established branches of Christianity — whether they are the Roman Catholic Church, mainline Protestantism, or otherwise. The millions in American society who reject established Christianity range from liberal New Agers to conservative evangelicals. On the left, there is huge interest in religious pluralism, with many modern seekers essentially customizing their own "religion" out of the various ideas they savor from the world's religious traditions. On the right, millions of Christians flock every Sunday to intentionally "nondenominational" churches — with casual contemporary worship, informal attitudes, multi-racial congregations, and clergy who deliberately avoid the traditional titles, trappings, or styles of ordained status. In a society deeply suspicious of ancient and established Christian churches, it is very easy to convince people that "what really happened" in church history is nothing like what "the priests" want you to believe. *The Da Vinci Code* capitalizes on these suspicions well.

Third, a great many people in our society are aware of the legacy of sexual, intellectual, and spiritual discrimination throughout church history. There is a huge interest in a greater variety of spirituality these days, as any observer of culture will attest. Much of that interest is in areas historically discouraged by the established churches — such as in feminist, natural, or other less "formal" approaches to divinity. *The Da Vinci Code* claims quite plainly that Jesus' true naturalist and feminist message was altogether different than what the "fathers taught." As such, the book has attracted a great deal of attention from those popular readers seeking to explore these fascinating areas of feminine and natural theology.

And fourth, there is an incredible lack of knowledge among people in contemporary society about western civilization's intellectual, religious, philosophical, and cultural history. These days, as observers from Barzun to Bennet have noted, many of us are bereft of any personal connection to the flow of events and ideas that existed before we were born. In a society addicted to popular culture, we are starved for the nourishment of thousands of years of world civilization and its vast stores of knowledge. People are aware of their hunger for ancient knowledge and understanding, but they really don't even know where to begin to find a good meal of it. So they devour intellectual snacks. People yearn for books that package even the *pretense* of cultural and spiritual literacy in a form they can easily swallow. *The Da Vinci Code*'s pretense of scholarship into a vast array of interesting categories is a big part of why the book has been so popular. As its early reviewers assured readers, "the book is filled with several doctorates' worth" of information and ideas. In a society that wants it all and wants it fast and knows it knows very little of the "higher" things, a book that can be read in two days and makes you feel as if you learned something is going to sell well — even if that book is little more than an intellectual and spiritual pop tart.

While it must be said *The Da Vinci Code* contains a load of bad information, it may also be said to contain that charismatic spark which helps to draw people to ideas and to theologies that too often go unexamined. For, as much as the book's many errors exasperated and offended me, I must praise Dan Brown for getting so many people interested in the Bible, Jesus, Mary

Magdalene, the sacred feminine, and Christian history. Because of Dan Brown, I've been a very busy priest, and that is a blessing indeed.

Afterword by Deirdre Good

PROFESSOR OF NEW TESTAMENT
THE GENERAL THEOLOGICAL SEMINARY

I understand that the genre of an "afterword" is to observe what has gone before and point to what is yet to come. Greg Jones' experience of being asked about the veracity of Dan Brown's phenomenally successful *The Da Vinci Code* must be a universal one for priests and ministers of institutional religion — not only in North America but also in Europe, Australia, and New Zealand. Anecdotally I can report that the book fascinates women and men equally. To be sure, groups of women engaged in their own spiritual journeys to whom I have spoken find in the book confirmation of their distrust of institutional religion and affirmation of the place of women, hitherto sup-pressed, perhaps with whom they identify. But men once active in religious life, even in orders, stayed behind to share private-ly their own suspicions of official institutional religion after presentations on the book in parishes in and around New York City in the fall of 2003 and the spring of 2004.

That *The Da Vinci Code* invites readers to ask questions and engage in their own interpretation of ancient material culture and Christian tradition is all to the good. Since the book models a deconstructive and reconstructive exercise simultaneously, it invites readers into a similar exercise. In this regard, its timing is exquisite. Coming right on the heels of the pedophile scandal in the Roman Catholic Church exposed first by the Boston Globe in 2002, one could imagine readers (particularly Roman Catholic ones) asking: "What else haven't we been told?" And readers who had never heard of the Gospel of Mary or Opus Dei could search for further information on the Internet from the comfort of their local library or even their homes.

Greg Jones sets the book against ancient texts together with historical reconstructions and interpretations of those texts. Against these, he finds *The Da Vinci Code* wanting. This is a reasonable response, and one could add to it critical questions about which historical interpretations *The Da Vinci Code* favors and why. After all, the book purports to be history. Assuming it is true, one might ask (as I have of readers) what difference does it make to your faith if Jesus and Mary Magdalene had a sexual relationship? For some people, it matters not a whit. In fact, they are gratified to perceive the extent of Jesus' humanity. For others, it seems scandalous.

To the factual errors of *The Da Vinci Code* Greg Jones identifies, I can add others. As far as we know from records of church councils, it is not true that eighty gospels were considered for the New Testament. The process of canonization, namely, of selecting which books would be considered canonical — that is, authoritative — took several hundred years. From these early centuries several lists survive, most notably that of Athanasius, who in 386 wrote an Easter letter identifying the books to be regarded as authoritative, the books to be used for private devotion, and the books to be excluded.

Nor is it true, as *The Da Vinci Code* claims, that Jesus' divinity was not established until the Council of Nicea. From writings of the New Testament like Pauline letters (Greg Jones cites the beautiful hymn to Christ in Philippians 2), and New Testament gospels, and other writings like the Revelation of St. John, together with writings from the patristic period, we can see clearly that diverse groups of Jesus' followers claimed his divinity. To be sure, how they did this and by what means, and what they claimed him to be (in addition to what he claimed he was) is a complicated and fascinating study. Nicca however represents an *evolution* in Christological discussions, not something out of the clear blue sky.

Most of what *The Da Vinci Code* says about the Dead Sea Scrolls is entirely wrong. Finally, the claim that Q was written by Jesus is simply not true. Q is a reconstructed sayings source that some scholars believe to have been used by Matthew and Luke in the composition of their gospels.

Beyond *Da Vinci* proposes to let the existing Catholic organization, Opus Dei, speak for itself. I think however, it behooves us to know something more about it. Unlike the Priory of Sion, Opus Dei is a worldwide organization of the Roman Catholic Church whose numbers in 1995 were estimated at 77,000 including fifteen hundred priests and fifteen bishops. *The Da Vinci Code* wrongly calls it a "sect." Intended to strengthen the presence of Catholic laity in the world as an extension of the salvific mission that the Church carries out for the life of the world, Opus Dei was made a personal prelature by the Holy See in 1982. This is a canonical term meaning that its jurisdiction covers the persons in Opus Dei, rather than a particular region. It operates in the same manner as religious orders, namely, without regard for geographical boundaries. Within the United States membership is estimated at three thousand, with sixty-four centers or residences for members in seventeen cities ("Opus Dei in the United States," James Martin, SJ, in *America* 1995). Opus Dei is an organization to watch and its recruitment practices have come under scrutiny.

Discussions of history notwithstanding, *The Da Vinci Code* is almost universally acknowledged as fiction. Thus, I'd like to propose other questions: what is the role and authority of historical fiction and what weight should we give to imagination in historical reconstruction? Finally, since the book interprets architecture and art, one might ask how and by what means do we "read" material culture including texts, symbols, and paintings (such as those of Leonardo) and who has the authority to do this?

I'll start with which historical interpretations *The Da Vinci Code* favors and why. In the case of Mary Magdalene, for example, one could see depictions in texts from the first two centuries of the Common Era in which she is apostle, prophet, visionary, evangelist, recipient of an exorcism, and so on, over against features emphasized by Dan Brown. While it is clear that *The Da Vinci Code* deliberately corrects the notion that Mary Magdalene was a prostitute in favor of her special relationship with Jesus, a correction that feminist scholarship has promulgated for some time, the novel also proposes that the special relationship that exists between Mary Magdalene and Jesus can only be interpreted as a sexual one in which they were married. To be sure, the character Leigh Teabing says:

"Jesus was the original feminist. He intended for the future of His Church to be in the hands of Mary Magdalene." This is a fascinating, if anachronistic reconstruction. But does the reader ever hear what the gospel of Mary Magdalene might be? Or what her theological insights were? Do we even hear her voice? No. In *The Da Vinci Code*, Mary Magdalene is only the repository of Jesus' seed and the object of a sacred quest. She may not be a prostitute, but neither is she an apostle or an evangelist. In other words, there is a great deal more that we now know about Mary Magdalene, starting with reports she gives of her vision as a consequence of the special relationship existing between them. And this information is accessible in current translations of ancient texts and books on Mary Magdalene, of which there are presently a large number in print.

Greg Jones is quite right to urge his readers to rediscover the sacred feminine in Christian and Jewish scriptures. For several decades feminist scholars like Carol Meyers (*Women in Scripture: A Dictionary of Named and Unnamed Women in the Hebrew Bible, the Apocryphal/Deuterocanonical Books and the New Testament*) and Phyllis Trible (*God and the Rhetoric of Sexuality* and *Texts of Terror*) have made accessible texts about women and female imagery read as sources of blessing and also bane. Some texts as a result of these readings have made their way into lectionaries and prayer books. Yet in the tradition of the Episcopal Church, inclusive imagery for God and Christ found in the writings of Julian of Norwich or Wisdom traditions appears mainly in supplementary texts unused by Sunday worshipers. The canticle in the Daily Office that celebrates the delivery of Israelites from the Egyptians at the Red Sea, based on Exodus 15 and attributed by scholars Frank Moore Cross and David Noel Freedman (whom no one could accuse of being feminists) to Miriam rather than to Moses, is still called "The Song of Moses" in The Book of Common Prayer. Much more needs to be done both in regard to bible translations, prayer books, and lectionary readings.

Greg Jones rightly points out that devotion to Mary, the mother of Jesus, is strangely ignored by The Da Vinci Code. Today we are seeing renewed interest in Mary in studies and collected essays published by Catholic and Protestant scholars like Elizabeth Johnson (Truly Our Sister: A Theology of Mary in the Communion of the Saints) and Beverly Gaventa (Blessed One: Protestant Perspectives on Mary). This interest shows no sign of abating and draws on Hebrew Scriptures, the New Testament, noncanonical texts like the Protevangelion of James and later eastern Orthodox texts, and the Qu'ran. Material on Mary traditions by scholars in Jewish, Christian, and Islamic traditions is forthcoming in a collection I have edited (Miriam, the Magdalen, and the Mother).

Next, what is the role and authority of historical fiction and what weight should we give to imagination in historical reconstruction? The Da Vinci Code demonstrates the power of historical fiction. It breathes life into arid and dry bones of ancient history. Critics of The Da Vinci Code may be able to demonstrate its historical inaccuracies, but what we are left with seems reliable yet dull. The question remains: can something sound and enthralling be written about the first two centuries of Christianity? Elaine Pagels' books from The Gnostic Gospels to Beyond Belief demonstrate that it is possible to write accessibly and reliably for a wide audience. No teacher can afford to ignore the access historical fiction gives to the past.

No one who has read books like Pat Barker's *The Ghost Road* and Sebastian Faulk's *Birdsong* can ever think of the Great War as a distant historical event of ninety years ago. Of course there is implausible historical fiction. "People of the past are not just us in odd clothing" writes Anne Scott MacLeod in *Horn Book Magazine*. This is especially true of the distant past. Even if human nature is much the same over time, human experience — perhaps especially everyday experience — and human values are not. To wash these differences out of historical fictions is a denial of historical truth. It is also a failure of imagination and understanding that is as important to the present as to the past. Even after Margaret George's *Mary, Called Magdalene: A Novel*, opportunities remain for scholars capable of writing simply and engagingly in ways that respect different experiences and values of the ancient world.

As I have said elsewhere (in Dan Burstein's *Secrets of the Code: The Unauthorized Guide to the Mysteries Behind The Da Vinci Code*), *The Da Vinci Code* uses fiction as a means to interpret historical obscurity. Fiction enables writers to supply sinews in historical material that can enflesh dry bones. Would it not be possible to write about the particular connection existing between Mary Magdalene and Jesus attested in ancient texts as a spiritual bond rather than a primarily physical one? Jane Shaberg (*The Resurrection of Mary Magalene: Legends, Apocrypha, and the Christian Testament*), Karen King (*The Gospel of Mary of Magdala: Jesus and the First Woman Apostle*), Ann Graham Brock (*Mary Magdalene, The First Apostle: The Struggle for Authority*), and Holly Hearon (*The Mary Magdalene Tradition*) have written excellent recent books on this topic. They provide material for reflection and further investigation.

The Da Vinci Code presents a world of symbols to the reader. As Paul Tillich wrote in *Dynamics of Faith*, symbols are found in every culture at every period of human history. Words are just as much symbols as national flags. Symbols however are multivalent, changing over time and place to connote multiple meanings and ideas. Moreover, they convey our deepest ideals and values. For those who understand the power of symbols, *The Da Vinci Code*'s use of the pentacle, the rose, and the Holy Grail evoke powerful traditions. And because symbols are variable and powerful, they convey an allure to readers unfamiliar with symbolic meanings. *The Da Vinci Code*, however, locks in specific meanings of these symbols: the rose is a symbol of female sexuality; Mary Magdalene as a receptacle is the Holy Grail. But these symbols are more powerful and nuanced than these specific meanings as Diane Apostolos-Cappadona points out in *Secrets of the Code*. Is it possible to write about symbols in such a way as to leave their meaning open and their power intact? J. R. R. Tolkein does this for the ring. In *Lord of the Rings* he depicts Frodo, the hero of the novel, as a ring-bearer (not wearer) on an epic journey to destroy the ring. Readers have only glimpses of the ring's power and its effect on those who wear it. By this technique, the untapped power of the ring remains potent until its destruction.

I hope these afterthoughts are read as invitations to participate in imaginative and responsible reconstructions of the period known as Christian Origins. To the extent that *Beyond Da Vinci* has engaged readers in this endeavor, it has succeeded, and for that we owe Greg Jones our thanks.

Bibliography

STANDARD REFERENCE

The Christian Theology Reader. Edited by Alister E. McGrath. Blackwell, 1995. An anthology of ancient, medieval, and modern theology that provides an overview of theological thinking from a wide range of perspectives, from early church Fathers to contemporary feminist and liberation theologians.

The Interpreter's Dictionary of the Bible. Abingdon Press, 1966. 17th printing, 1989. The articles in this four volume collection offer a historical-critical approach to the Bible and its themes.

New Catholic Encyclopedia, 1967. Vol. IX. Articles on Mary, the Mother of Jesus, offer an excellent introduction into Roman Catholic thought about Mary "the Blessed Virgin."

The Oxford Dictionary of the Christian Church. Oxford University Press, 3rd ed. 1997. A one-volume reference work for anyone interested in Christian history and practice.

The Oxford Dictionary of Saints. Oxford University. Press, 4th ed. 1997.

SCRIPTURAL COLLECTIONS

The Complete Dead Sea Scrolls in English. Geza Vermes. Allen Lane/The Penguin Press, 1997 ed. A standard collection of these valuable Old Testament and intertestamental texts.

The Interlinear NASB-NIV: Parallel New Testament in Greek and English. Zondervan, 1993. This is a handy tool for reading the New Testament in as "original" a version as possible.

The Nag Hammadi Library in English. Edited by James M. Robinson. 3rd rev. ed. HarperSanFrancisco, 1988. The definitive translation of the Gnostic scriptures in English.

The Old Testament Pseudoepigrapha, vols. 1&2. Doubleday, 1983. A fascinating collection of ancient Jewish writings not included in any biblical canon.

The Septuagint with Apocrypha: Greek and English. Translated by Sir Lancelot C. L. Breton. Hendrickson, 2001. This is the Greek language version of the Old Testament and the Apocrypha. It was produced by the Greek-speaking Jews of Egypt in the third century before Christ.

WRITINGS FROM ANTIQUITY

Ambrose. *Funeral Oration for Theodosius.* (A number of translations are available.) A late fourth-century comparison of Helena Augusta, mother of Augustine, with Mary, the mother of Jesus.

Egeria. *Diary of a Pilgrimage.* Translated by George E. Gingras. Newman Press, 1970. The detailed itinerary of a Roman woman to the Holy Land in the fourth century.

Eusebius. *The History of the Church from Christ to Constantine.* Penguin Books, 1989. A handy student's paperback edition of this early third-century work.

Eusebius. *The Life of Constantine.* From Nicene and Post-Nicene Fathers, vol. 1. Second Series. Hendrickson Publishers, 1994. A classic edition first published in the late nineteenth century.

Grant, Robert M. *Second-Century Christianity: A Collection of Fragments.* 2nd ed. Westminster John Knox Press, 2003. A very helpful collection of pagan, Christian, and Gnostic primary texts.

Richardson, Cyril C. *Early Christian Fathers.* Touchstone, 1996. A collection of ancient Christian writings from the first two centuries of the Common Era.

SCHOLARLY BOOKS

Barzun, Jacques. *From Dawn to Decadence: 500 Years of Western Cultural Life.* HarperCollinsPublishers, 2000. An epic work for the non-specialized general reader.

Borgehammar, Stephan. *How the Holy Cross was Found: From Event to Medieval Legend: With an Appendix of Texts.* Stockholm: Almqvist & Wiksell, 1991. Borgehammar's doctoral thesis is hard to find, but is a new and highly influential reexamination of the life and times of Constantine, the Holy Land, and Helena Augustus.

Chadwick, Henry. *The Early Church.* Rev. ed. Penguin, 1993. A scholarly summary of early church history intended for the general reader.

Drijvers, Jan Willem. *Helena Augusta: The Mother of Constantine the Great and the Legend of her Finding of the True Cross.* Leiden; New York: E.J. Brill, 1992. Another hard-to-find doctoral thesis and, like Borgehammar's book, a highly influential new scholarly examination of Constantine, Helena Augusta, and the Holy Land.

Gibbon, Edward. *The History of the Decline and Fall of the Roman Empire.* Abridged. Penguin Books, 2000. The "industry standard" text on late Roman antiquity for over two centuries, beautifully written from a highly skeptical Enlightenment perspective.

Hunt, E. D. *Holy Land Pilgrimage in the Later Roman Empire, AD 312-460.* Oxford University Press, 1982. A fascinating scholarly examination of pilgrims to the Holy Land in the 300s. We learn about Helena, the Pilgrim of Bordeaux, and many others.

Jones, A. H. M., *The Later Roman Empire, 284-602: A Social, Economic, and Administrative Survey.* (2 vols. Johns Hopkins University Press, 1986. An exhaustive two-volume study, better for the serious academic than for the general reader.

Nachef, Antoine. *Mary's Pope: John Paul II, Mary, and the Church since Vatican II.* Sheed & Ward, 2000. A thorough study of Marian theology and the Roman Catholic Church.

Pelikan, Jaroslav. *The Christian Tradition.* 5 vols. University of Chicago Press, 1971. This is an excellent scholarly work by a Yale scholar for undergraduate and graduate level readers.

Rudolph, Kurt. *Gnosis: The Nature and History of Gnosticism.* Translated by Robert McLachlan Wilson. HarperSanFrancisco, 1987. This is the definitive book on the subject from a preeminent scholarly authority.

Wallace-Hadrill, J. M. *The Frankish Church.* Oxford University Press, 1983. Perhaps the best recent scholarly appraisal of Christianity in France from the Roman through the Merovingian and Carolingian periods.

Williams, Rowan. *Arius: Heresy & Tradition*. Rev. ed. Wm. B. Eerdmans Publishing Co., 2002. A dense but rewarding examination of Arius and Arianism, written before the author became Archbishop of Canterbury.

Young, Frances. *The Making of the Creeds*. Trinity International, 1991. One of the best short scholarly studies of the development of the Nicene and other ancient Christian creeds. Her work is clear and concise.

POPULAR BOOKS, ARTICLES, AND
TELEVISION PROGRAMS

Andersen, Wayne. *Freud, Leonardo Da Vinci, and the Vulture's Tail: A Refreshing Look at Leonardo's Sexuality*. Karnac, 2001.

Baigent, Michael; Richard Leigh; and Henry Lincoln. *Holy Blood, Holy Grail*. Dell, 1983.

BBC Timewatch Series. *The History of a Mystery*. BBC television, 1996.

Boucher, Bruce. "Does 'The Da Vinci Code' Crack Leonardo?" *The New York Times*. 3 August 2003.

Brown, Dan. *The Da Vinci Code*. Doubleday, 2003.

De Imperatoribus Romanis: An Online Encyclopedia of Roman Emperors, www.roman-emperors.org. Provides useful biographical sketches of all Roman Emperors.

Ehrman, Bart D. *Lost Christianities: The Battles for Scripture and the Faiths We Never Knew*. Oxford University Press, 2003.

Eisenman, Robert. *James the Brother of Jesus: The Key to Unlocking the Secrets of Early Christianity and the Dead Sea Scrolls*. Penguin, 1997.

Frontline Series. *From Jesus to Christ: the First Christians*. WGBH Educational Foundation, 1998. Broadcast on PBS. Available on Warner Home Video. Television series which explores Jesus "and the movement he started." Professor Elizabeth Clark of Duke University is interviewed in this series.

Gardner, Laurence. *Bloodline of the Holy Grail: The Hidden Lineage of Jesus Revealed*. Barnes & Noble Books, 1997.

King, Karen. "Letting Mary Magdalene Speak." Published online at http://www.beliefnet.com/story/131/story_13186.html.

Miller, Laura. "The Da Vinci Con", *The New York Times,* 22 February 2004.

Mizrach, Steven. "Priory of Sion: The Facts, The Theories, The Mystery." Article written by Florida International University adjunct professor Dr. Steven Mizrach. He sent me this article by e-mail.

Pagels, Elaine. *The Gnostic Gospels.* Vintage Books, 1989.

Persaud, Dr. Raj. "Genius on Genius? Freud on Leonardo da Vinci." Published on the web at http://www.psychologypsychiatry.com.

Picknett, Lynn, and Clive Prince. *The Templar Revelation.* Touchstone, 1998.

Ralls, Karen. *The Templars and the Grail.* Quest Books, 2003.

Richardson, Robert. "The Priory of Sion Hoax." *Gnosis,* No. 51, Spring, 1999. This was the last issue of *Gnosis,* the special Holy Grail issue. On the web, go to: www.lumen.org.

Smith, Paul. "Priory of Sion — The Pierre Plantard Archives — 1937-1993. Go directly to Paul Smith's archives through my own web domain: www.prioryofsion.org.

Witherington, Ben III. "Mary, Mary, Extraordinary." Published online at http://www.beliefnet.com/story/135/story_13503.html.

Woodward, Kenneth L. "A Quite Contrary Mary." Published online at http://www.beliefnet.com/story/131/story_13188.html.

NOTES

CHAPTER 1

1. *Newsweek International*, October 7, 2002, "Opus Dei in the Open."
2. The Priory of Sion hoax is outlined in the Spring 1999 issue of *Gnosis*, an esoteric magazine dedicated to the exploration of New Age themes. In an article called "The Priory of Sion Hoax," Robert Richardson debunked the whole idea a few years before *The Da Vinci Code* was published.
3. Karen Ralls, *The Templars and the Grail*, Quest Books, 2003, 42. This book is a fascinating but overly credulous piece of work. As far as "Grail Lore" goes, Ralls' book is a quality work in an esoteric genre normally impoverished of credible scholarship.
4. In 1009 the Church of the Holy Sepulcher was destroyed by Egyptian Sultan al-Hakim. His men may have damaged the Church of Our Lady of Zion as well.
5. These facts appear in two French texts: *Mythologie du trésor de Rennes* by René Descadeillas in 1974 and *Autopsie d'un mythe* by Jean-Jacques Bedu in 1990.

CHAPTER 2

1. Bruce Boucher, "Does 'The Da Vinci Code' Crack Leonardo?" *New York Times*, 3 August 2003
2. Jacques Barzun, *From Dawn to Decadence: 500 Years of Western Cultural Life*, Harper Collins Publishers, 76.

CHAPTER 3

1. Mark 2:21-28
2. Luke 10:25-37
3. Acts 17:22-25

4. Chadwick, 128.
5. The draft creed declared that the Father and the Son were "of one substance," but this might mean that they were specifically identical, or generically identical. Indeed, centuries of subsequent disagreement over a different phrase in the Creed, "who proceeds from the Father and the Son," would become the pretext for the schism between the western and eastern branches of the church seven centuries later.

CHAPTER 4

1. K. Rudolph, *Gnosis*, 154.
2. Gospel of Thomas, *The Nag Hammadi Library*, 114.
3. *Gnosis*, 367.
4. *The Nag Hammadi Library*, 2-3.
5. I was surprised to find in Elaine Pagels' *The Gnostic Gospels* the Gospel of Philip quotation just as it appears in *The Da Vinci Code* – and she claims to be citing directly from *The Nag Hammadi Library*. When I checked her footnote for the citation with my copy of *The Nag Hammadi Library*, her purported quotation does *not* match up with what is actually there. It appears that Pagels has *added the controversial* bracketed words herself – a fact which if true is very troubling coming from a scholar of her stature. See Pagels' *Gnostic Gospels*, p. xv, and corresponding note on p. 153.

CHAPTER 5

1. Pagels, 48.
2. *The Interpreter's Dictionary of the Bible*, vol. 4, 317-18.

CHAPTER 6

1. *The Da Vinci Code*, 125. That number is a tremendous exaggeration. The woman's human rights group, Gendercide, tracks past and present abuses against women. They estimate that church inquisitions killed between thirty-five and sixty thousand individuals as witches over three centuries, of which a large percentage were men.